D1470304

"There is a yearning today for a faith that is real, deep, and authentic. It wants to keep marketing at arm's length and to escape from cultural compromises because both are pathways into superficiality and emptiness. This book addresses that yearning with clarity and conviction and, along the way, connects its readers with what Christians in their best moments have always believed."

—DAVID WELLS, Distinguished Research Professor, Gordon-Conwell Theological Seminary

PROCLAIMING A
CROSS-CENTERED THEOLOGY

Other books by
Together for the Gospel:

Preaching the Cross (2007)

TOGETHER FOR THE GOSPEL

PROCLAIMING A CROSS-CENTERED THEOLOGY

Mark Dever, J. Ligon Duncan III,
R. Albert Mohler Jr., C. J. Mahaney

Contributions by John MacArthur, John Piper,
R. C. Sproul, Thabiti Anyabwile

CROSSWAY WHEATON, ILLINOIS

Proclaiming a Cross-centered Theology

Copyright © 2009 by Together for the Gospel

Published by Crossway Books
        a publishing ministry of Good News Publishers
        1300 Crescent Street
        Wheaton, Illinois 60187

Cover design: Cindy Kiple

Cover illustration: iStock

First printing 2009

Printed in the United States of America

Scripture quotations marked ESV are from the ESV® Bible (*The Holy Bible, English Standard Version®*), copyright © 2001 by Crossway Bibles, a publishing ministry of Good News Publishers. Used by permission. All rights reserved.

Scripture quotations marked KJV are from the *King James Version* of the Bible.

Scripture quotations marked NASB are from *The New American Standard Bible®*. Copyright © The Lockman Foundation 1960, 1962, 1963, 1968, 1971, 1972, 1973, 1975, 1977, 1995. Used by permission.

Scripture references marked NIV are from *The Holy Bible: New International Version®*. Copyright © 1973, 1978, 1984 by International Bible Society. Used by permission of Zondervan Publishing House. All rights reserved.

The "NIV" and "New International Version" trademarks are registered in the United States Patent and Trademark Office by International Bible Society. Use of either trademark requires the permission of International Bible Society.

Scripture references marked NKJV are from *The New King James Version*. Copyright © 1982, Thomas Nelson, Inc. Used by permission.

All emphases in Scripture have been added by the authors.

Hardcover ISBN: 978-1-4335-0206-4

PDF ISBN: 978-1-4335-1251-3

Mobipocket ISBN: 978-1-4335-1252-0

ePub ISBN: 978-1-4335-2218-5

Library of Congress Cataloging-in-Publication Data
Proclaiming a cross-centered theology / Mark Dever . . . [et al.].
   p. cm.
  Includes index.
  ISBN 978-1-4335-0206-4 (hc)
  1. Preaching. 2. Theology of the cross. I. Dever, Mark. I. Title.
BV4211.3.P76   2009
251—dc22   2009012177

LB		19	18	17	16	15	14	13	12	11	10	09
15	14	13	12	11	10	9	8	7	6	5	4	3	2	1

To the rising generation of
theologians of the cross

CONTENTS

INTRODUCTION

The great English preacher C. H. Spurgeon recounted one of the more unusual experiences of his highly unusual life. He was headed to Haverhill in Suffolk and, due to rail delays, was running late for a preaching engagement. I'll let him pick up the story here:

> So it happened that I reached the appointed place considerably behind time. Like sensible people, they had begun their worship, and had proceeded as far as the sermon. As I neared the chapel, I perceived that someone was in the pulpit preaching, and who should the preacher be but my dear and venerable grandfather! He saw me as I came in at the front door, and made my way up the aisle, and at once he said, "Here comes my grandson! He may preach the gospel better than I can, but he cannot preach a better gospel; can you, Charles?" As I pressed through the throng, I answered, "You can preach better than I can. Pray go on." But he would not agree to *that*. I must take the sermon, and so I did, going on with the subject there and then, just where he left off.[1]

That great gospel is the subject of this volume (and the Together for the Gospel Conference at which a spoken version of these chapters was first presented). This volume is prepared with the assumption that there is widespread agreement about the gospel across denominational lines, but also with the conviction that the gospel is widely under attack. Some of those assaults are deliberate and intended; others are not. Some are subtle; others are obvious frontal assaults. It is with a love primarily for the gospel that these messages were given. And it is with this same love that they are now brought together and presented to you.

The participants were given a free hand to choose and frame their own messages. We have all been a part of conversations and discussions about these issues, many with one another. We have all felt the need to contend for these matters. The tone of this conference was defensive, in the sense that pastoral work is partly defensive—defending the sheep against wolves in sheep's clothing. Building the church has always involved the sword along with the trowel. Contention and contradiction is a necessary part of preaching, as all faithful pastors know. While some may love such fights, we intend to love the gospel. It is because of that love—not a mere love of fighting and contending itself—that we are willing to contend for these matters.

When Erasmus wrote his quasi-irenic treatise *On the Freedom of the Will*, he wrote, "I take no delight in assertions." Luther responded in Lutherly fashion:

> It is not the mark of a Christian mind to take no delight in assertions; on the contrary, a man must delight in assertions or he will be no Christian. And by assertion . . . I mean a constant adhering, affirming, confessing, maintaining, and an invincible persevering. . . . Nothing is better known or more common among Christians than assertion. Take away assertions and you take away Christianity. Why, the Holy Spirit is given them from heaven, that a Christian may glorify Christ and confess him even unto death—unless it is not asserting when one dies for one's confession and assertion.[2]

It is in a Luther-like sense of confessing that the preachers contributing to this volume offer these assertions.

Ligon Duncan begins this volume as he began that conference. He entered the lists asserting that systematic theology is a worthwhile task. Indeed, in days when the narrative form of biblical theology is attracting great (and deserved) attention, it is too often being pitted against systematic theology. Ligon defends the usefulness and necessity of systematic theology with clarity and vigor. A pastor must remember the truths in this chapter or risk losing the gospel itself.

Next up is Thabiti Anyabwile. Thabiti was new to the Together for the Gospel (T4G) conference as a speaker. He has been a friend of most of ours for years, being a member and elder at Capitol Hill Baptist Church and now the pastor of First Baptist Church, Grand Cayman. We have shared conferences and weekends with him and have been instructed by his teaching and edified by the testimony of God's amazing grace in his life. (Before his conversion, Thabiti was a nationally recognized college speaker on African-American studies. He had also been a practicing Muslim.) In his address at Together for the Gospel, Thabiti challenged us to recognize that the category of "race" is irredeemable. It brings far more confusion than light, more contention than understanding, more prejudice than impartial judgment. As you turn to that chapter—perhaps the most explosive of the conference—open your mind and get ready to think.

John MacArthur delivered a message on human depravity that was a model of clear thinking. In it, John masterfully assembled the witness of Scripture (in the very way Ligon had encouraged us the previous day) on this vital topic. John showed that a mistake here is a mistake in the foundation of understanding the nature of our problem. He laid out challenges currently facing this doctrine and concluded by calling us to be faithful to this aspect of the message, no matter how hard we may find such faithfulness.

The next message was mine. I had been mulling over for some time the confusion about the content of the gospel. The message came together as I reviewed notes I had made some months earlier about various issues that needed "addressing." I began to notice that each one evidenced a distortion of the gospel. With encouragement from my T4G brothers—and the Capitol Hill Baptist congregation—I worked and reworked the material until I felt I got close to saying what I wanted to say. I wanted to get evangelicals talking about what the gospel is exactly. Of course, they were having that conversation before this message was given, but I wanted to add my voice to the call for clarity on the gospel. What is the core of the gospel? And how important is clarity on that core? I wanted to encourage a continuing priority on evangelism in the local church. I said to friends at the time that I understood that "gospel" could be used in a broader sense, but I was speaking about the heart of it, without which no other news is "good news." In order to bring further clarity, I've appended a wonderful brief piece by Greg Gilbert on exactly this point.

R. C. Sproul brought to the conference what many felt was the most devotionally rich meditation on the sacrifice of Christ. And he did it by meditating upon the curse motif in the Old Testament! In his own inimitable conversational style, with wide learning and profound biblical understanding, R. C. took us on a tour of Old Testament practices, verbally painting scenes before our eyes. Again and again, as we stared into the depth of those practices, we began to see the cross of Christ more and more clearly until, well, let me simply encourage you to read what I heard many call "the best I've ever heard R. C." And, I promise—it's not R. C. you'll be glorifying when you're done.

During the second night of the conference, Al Mohler brought a new depth of care to the topic of the atonement. This conference in many ways was birthed out of our concern that the atonement is being misconceived and mistaught in too many evangelical books and churches. It was Al who decided to wade into the sea of literature and explain to us what has happened. With a mastery of the literature that is both exceptional and yet typical of our well-read friend, he led us to see the lines of misunderstanding—of attack— that have been laid down against Christ's death being in the place of sinners. His conference message, now here in print, should serve as a guide to the literature and, even more fundamentally, to thinking carefully about the atoning work of Christ.

The last day of the conference, John Piper brought the cross into our own lives and ministries. He posed the question, "How does the supremacy of Christ create radical Christian sacrifice?" Looking through the last few chapters of Hebrews, John called for us to live radical lives so as to have radical ministries. He called us to be God's men. He called us to be certain that in such a ministry suffering will come. He inspired us with the example of the late Sir Norman Anderson, a brilliant Christian scholar in London who taught Islamic law for years and who suffered a great deal in his life, though without apparent bitterness. (I had the privilege of knowing Sir Norman a bit, and he was as strikingly kind as he was brilliant.) John helped us examine what caused such willingness to suffer, and he turned us to the Savior to see how Christ's person and saving work is displayed in our suffering. As a result, I, along with many others, felt compelled to follow Christ "outside the camp." We pray that you will resolve to do the same as you meditate on this chapter.

The final message was once again given by the conference pastor C. J. Mahaney. C. J. preached a wonderful message titled "Sustaining the Pastor's Soul." He presented Paul as an example of one who suffered without complaint and served with obvious joy, regardless of the circumstances. And he called us to be "happy pastors," too. What was it he repeatedly said? "How striking that the one with the most responsibility was the one with the most joy." Many times since hearing this, when I have been tempted to complain, I have thought of Paul's example and been rebuked and, as C. J. would say, "adjusted." Looking at Paul's letter to the Philippians, C. J. helped us consider Paul's foundational gratitude to God, his continuing faith in God, and finally, and most convictingly, his love for others. C. J. brings the great commands to love God and neighbor specifically to the pastoral ministry through the example of the great apostle. Even though this message appears as the book's last chapter, if you're a pastor and feeling particularly pressed, let me suggest that you begin there.

Well, what remains now is for you to read the volume and be built up. Thank God for his faithfulness to his covenant, even to the point of Christ's death on the cross. This is good news indeed!

—Mark Dever, October 2008, for Ligon Duncan,
Albert Mohler, and C. J. Mahaney

CHAPTER 1

SOUND DOCTRINE: ESSENTIAL TO FAITHFUL PASTORAL MINISTRY

A Joyful Defense and Declaration of the Necessity and Practicality of Systematic Theology for the Life and Ministry of the Church

J. Ligon Duncan III

We live and minister in an anti-doctrinal age or, at least, an age that thinks it's anti-doctrinal. We live and minister in an age that is anti-theological, or at least it claims to be anti-theological. By that, I mean that it is now the *zeitgeist* to claim to be suspicious of doctrine, doctrinal systems, and systematic theology all the while holding to one's own cherished doctrines and system emphatically, if unwittingly and inchoately. But this spirit of our age gets us started down the wrong track in discussing doctrine and the Christian life, and systematic theology and ministry. This outlook gets us into a debate about whether we ought to be doctrinal in our ministry, or whether we ought to be less confident in our doctrine, or whether we ought to be more biblical and less doctrinal, or whether we ought to be more "narratival" or "storied" and less didactic and systematic.

Why Dubiety of Doctrine Doesn't Work

There are at least three problems with starting the discussion this way. It misdiagnoses our culture, our problem, and the relation of Scripture to theology. First, it assumes that our culture is non- or anti-doctrinal. It isn't. It just thinks it is. You will find its vehement doctrines hidden in its ethics and narratives. Touch its ethics, and you will find how very quickly it will get doctrinal (try this out on a "non-doctrinal" member of NARAL, and then see how quickly the doctrine of "a woman's right to choose" comes up). Second, it locates our problem in the very concepts of doctrine and systematic theology, as if one could be doctrine-less or system-less. You can't. Everyone has doctrine and everyone has a system, especially those who howl most loudly that they don't and that they don't like propositions and systems. Third, it assumes that you can choose to approach the Scripture in a way that is exegetical and non-doctrinal, or narratival and non-systematic. You can't. Scripture itself explicitly asserts theological propositions and necessarily entails doctrinal formulation and systematic theology. So to even start the discussion of doctrine and pastoral ministry in a "postmodern" way is mostly unhelpful.

Instead, we need to look to the Scriptures to learn how doctrine informs, is necessary to, and is essential for faithful pastoral ministry if we are going to respond effectively to the anti-doctrinal, anti-theological spirit of the age in our gospel proclamation, and if we are going to edify the church with the meat of the Word. We need to understand the objections of our time, to be sure. We need to understand the doctrinal shortcomings of the past and present, yes. We need to hear the doubts of the postmoderns and understand them, but then we need to give a better diagnosis and prescription than they themselves have offered.

A Threefold Discussion

For the sake of clarity, allow me to tell you ahead of time what I want to argue in this chapter. First, *I want to argue that the very ideas of doctrine, theology, and systematic theology are under great duress in our time.* There are many people (even people who call themselves evangelical) who call into question the legitimacy of the whole project of systematic theology, who are dubious about the importance and nature of theology and wonder about the useful-ness of doctrine in the life of the church. As faithful Bible-believing Christians and shepherds, we need to resist to the death falling under the influence of this mind-set. It is soul-killing and ministry-killing.

Yes, some are saying we need to meet postmodernism by embracing postmodern vagueness and uncertainty, but I want to suggest to you that, instead, we need to meet this mood, this trend, by celebrating truth, doctrine, and systematic theology. I want to suggest that your preaching needs to be both deliber-ately expositional and profoundly theological (John Piper and D. Martyn Lloyd-Jones provide two very different but equally help-ful examples of this). I want to urge you to be joyfully and emphati-cally doctrinal and theological in your faith, life, and ministry.

Second, *I want to show you from Scripture that systematic theology is necessary, important, and, in fact, unavoidable.* This is significant because many believe that systematic theology (in addi-tion to being an unbiblical, philosophical exercise) is unnecessary and unimportant and ought to be avoided at all costs. I want to convince you that everyone is a systematic theologian (whether they admit it or not—especially those who protest most loudly that they don't believe in systematic theology). The only question is whether we will be biblical in our systematic theology or make it up as we go along. And I want you to see the value of systematic theology. I want you to see that your life is an extension of your systematic the-ology and doctrine. You are what you believe. If your life does not adorn your biblical doctrine, it suggests not that the Bible's doctrine is untrue but that at some profound level, that truth has not taken hold of you yet. It ought to be our aim to out-live, out-rejoice, and out-die the critics of theology and doctrine—to adorn our doctrine with our lives.

Third, *I want to identify in the Bible some things that systematic theology (in general) and doctrine (in particular) are important for.* The Bible itself, in the Old Testament and the New, makes clear that doctrine is for living. The study of doctrine is not (or at least ought not to be) an arid, speculative, impractical enterprise. Doctrine is for life! If the truth does not mold the way we live and minister, if it does not inform our speech, our relationships, our prayer, our worship, and our ministry, then the truth has gone bad on us—no matter how true the truth is. Biblical truth is meant to be expressed in our experience and practice, if we truly understand and believe it.

So, that's it. That's all I want to do in this chapter: (1) to alert you to an unhealthy contemporary attitude—doctrine, theology, and systematic theology are under great suspicion in the church today; (2) to demonstrate from the Bible that systematic theology is a biblical discipline (not an alien philosophical imposition on the Bible), and that doctrine and theology are important; and (3) to look at some specific biblical examples of what doctrine is important for.

1) Doctrine under Duress

We begin, then, with the attitude that has brought the concepts and legitimacy of doctrine, theology, and systematic theology (ST) under great duress in our own time.

The very ideas of theological propositions, doctrine, and especially systematic theology, are held in great suspicion today, even in the church. We hear even evangelicals around us saying things like "Christianity is a life, not a doctrine" (perhaps not knowing that it was nineteenth-century liberals who coined that phrase). By the way, you should read J. Gresham Machen's *Christianity and Liberalism* in which he gives an impressive biblical rejoinder to that assertion. It is one of ten books that every Protestant minister or ministerial candidate ought to read.[1]

People versus Truth

Meanwhile, others are telling us that we need to care less about our theology and more about people. I still remember a professor of mine telling me years ago, "People are more important than truth," which is itself, by the way, a proposition or truth claim. He was responding to the kind of impetuous theological gun-slinging mode of some seminarians who upon commencement are ready to dive-bomb an unsuspecting local congregation with biblical truth. But the biblical correction to the pastoral problem he was addressing is never, ever to diminish the importance of truth or teaching or doctrine but to know what truth is for.

God in his love gives his truth to us for our well-being. God's truth serves not only the interests of his own glory but also his people's good. Truth is for our everlasting joy in God. Furthermore, truth worked deep down into the heart and soul and bones of a preacher and then worked out in his relationships makes him tender and humble in his dealing with the sheep and in proclaiming and explaining the Word. So, though my professor's counsel was well-meaning and prompted by a genuine and legitimate pastoral concern, it was utterly wrongheaded.

Deeds over Creeds

We hear today the motto "Deeds, not creeds." The trouble is, we are hearing that not from Unitarian universalists (who invented the slogan, as far as I can tell), but from major evangelical leaders and from seminarians and from people in the pews of ostensibly evangelical churches. It's in the air. The mood the motto represents gets expressed in various ways: "Let's stop debating the faith and start living it." "Let's stop discussing theology and start doing it." Indeed, the hidden assumption behind these assertions is that understanding the truth is unrelated (and perhaps a positive hindrance) to the practice of the truth.

Person, Not Propositions

Listen to folks talk or lurk a bit on the Internet and you'll encounter an allergy to truth expressed in propositional form. Some express this with statements like "Christianity is a person, not a proposition" (the irony of this, again, is that it's a propositional statement); "Belief in absolute, universal truth is a modernist point of view and inherently rationalistic"; "Truth is personal and relational and takes place only in community"; and "Rational and propositional argumentation water down the gospel."

Systematic Theology Is Rationalist/Modernist

Much closer to home you will find a prejudice against doctrinal systems or the very project of systematic theology. Sometimes this is done by directly challenging the legitimacy of systematic theology: "Systematic theology is just proof-texting" or "Systematic theology is embellishing and harmonizing what the Bible says and then claiming that the Bible teaches our embellishment or harmonization." Sometimes systematic theology is challenged by criticizing the way it has been done in the past and because of the philosophical influences upon systematic theologians: "The Princetonians' ST was, unbeknownst to them, influenced and compromised by enlightenment rationalism and foundationalism due to Scottish commonsense realism." I chuckle when I hear people today who are themselves urging us to embrace "postmodernism," whatever that is, indignantly dismissing the Princetonians because of their "modernism."

Biblical Theology instead of Systematic Theology

In the meantime one also encounters a suspicion of ST from those who prefer "biblical theology," by which they generally mean a redemptive-historical approach to the Scriptures rather than a synthetic, topical approach. This critique has its slogans too: "ST is unbiblical. We need a theology that's more sensitive to narrative"; "God didn't give us a doctrinal system. He told us stories"; "We need more exegesis and less theology"; and "ST squeezes the biblical text into an alien framework and makes it answer questions that it was not written to answer."

Examples

Just so you don't think I'm crying wolf, let me give you just a few examples of these tendencies.

DOING, NOT DEBATING

You'll not be surprised to hear a Unitarian universalist minister say, "Religious liberals put less emphasis on formal beliefs and more on practical living. Our interest is in deeds, not creeds. We appreciate the biblical text, 'Be ye doers of the word, and not hearers only.'" But when a major evangelical figure who is otherwise orthodox says, "We need a reformation not of creeds but of deeds, so it's time to stop debating the Bible and start doing it," you know that something is in the water.

DANGEROUS DOCTRINE

The Saturday before T4G convened in Louisville in 2008, a major daily newspaper carried a religion article by a respected Jewish rabbi entitled, "The Dangers of Theology: Jews Focus More on Deed than Creed." Here's a taste (because it so well catches the current mood): "Theology. What a tricky thing. A devious thing, sometimes. A dangerous thing, often. Perhaps that is why Jews focus so much on deed and not creed, on doing rather than believing. It doesn't mean that Jews don't have faith; our faith is found in our actions."[2] At least three things need to be said about this quote.

(1) There is nothing unique to Judaism about this outlook; you find it everywhere in classically liberal theological circles. A liberal Catholic or Protestant—Episcopalian, Presbyterian, Baptist,

Methodist, Lutheran, or Congregationalist—could have said it. A wise, old, conservative Jewish professor of mine once told us with a twinkle in his eye, "A liberal Protestant, a liberal Catholic, and a liberal Jew can agree on almost everything, because they believe almost nothing!"

(2) What is interesting about the quote, the article, and the viewpoint is that we can find affinity for them within quadrants of evangelicalism, and not only in the more leftward leaning emergent circles.

(3) Even after eschewing theology and theologizing, the good rabbi cannot avoid doing it. Indeed, she goes on to say, "I officiated at a funeral on Sunday . . . [and] the family wanted me to speak about why bad things happen to good people. In other words, what is the cause of evil?"[3] The rest of the article is about how she tried to answer that question, and do you know what that required her to do? That's right: theology! What do you think was the very next word she wrote? Again you are right: "Theology." Here's what she went on to say: "Theology. How does a Jew respond to theology? It is a tough question, because there is no 'theology' in Judaism; there are only multiple theologies. Who is to say which one is right and which one is wrong? In fact, who is to say that they can't all be right at the same time?"[4]

I cannot resist pointing out that saying that there is no theology but rather multiple theologies in Judaism is itself a definite, debatable theological assertion. The minute you've said it, even if you think you've just dissed theology, you've in fact engaged in it, albeit poorly. Here's how she goes about tackling the issue of "why bad things happen to good people":

> So what do Jewish theologies say about the problem of evil? (Besides the fact that it is a problem?) Nothing satisfactory. . . . I tend to borrow a little from one philosopher here and another one there, as I build my own "recipe" for theology. Jews are allowed to do this, as long as we stay within particular theological

boundaries—strict monotheism being one of them, the idea that the Messiah has not yet come being the other.[5]

THE SELF-CONTRADICTIVE CRITIQUE

The confusions and contradictions here leave my head spinning. Seventeen simultaneous thoughts explode in my mind, but let me share just three of them. First, having previously asserted an utter theological relativism, the rabbi now admits two unquestionable and essential theological propositions without the slightest attempt to justify them on her own terms (and without the least sense of embarrassment).

Second, it apparently does not cross her mind that her admission of the existence of absolute theological boundary markers in her community and even her own ad-libbed attempt to answer the grieving family's question jointly call into question the very point she is making in the article.

Third, reading this reminded me of the story that Mark Dever tells in his book *Nine Marks of a Healthy Church*, in the second chapter on biblical theology. Mark was leading a seminar at an evangelical seminary, and after he had given a scriptural exposition of the doctrine of God, a classmate, Bill, objected and said that he likes to think of God rather differently. Mark writes, "For several minutes, Bill painted a picture for us of a very friendly deity. He liked to think of God as being wise, but not meddling; compassionate, but never overpowering; ever so resourceful, but never interrupting. 'This,' Bill said in conclusion, 'is how I like to think of God.'" Then Mark replied, "Thank you, Bill, for telling us so much about yourself, but we are concerned to know what God is really like, not simply about our own desires."[6] However, I digress.

What's Behind the Allergy?

It would be very easy for us to pillory and caricature what Rabbi Cohen wrote, but we ought first to read her argument sympathetically and attempt to understand why Cohen and so many other modern Jews (not to mention deconstructionists, in general) feel this way about theology. It is, at least in part, because they have seen bad theology kill. They understand that truth, or at least what is purported to be truth, can kill. And so they have gone the route of rejecting and relativizing truth. They have made the very understandable maneuver of reducing theology to the level of opinion in order to render it benign. Six million Jews lost their lives in Germany to the Nazis' bad theology. We could say the same of Stalin's and Mao's victims. And, on a different level, we can think of the discrimination and alienation that American Jews have experienced in our own culture.

You see how the argument goes. People have asserted truths with a capital T that have hurt and killed other people, so we are going to get rid of truth with a capital T. Period. But that is to make a tragically wrong response to a great evil. Bad theology kills. So get rid of the adjective, not the noun. Ditch the bad. Keep the theology. But the rabbi's solution is to reject the theology (or at least to relativize it), rather than to reject the bad.

This reminds me of an encounter I had with a Russian history professor in college who opined that the Bolsheviks were just like the Puritans. I perked up. What possible commonality could there be between Bolsheviks and Puritans? Well, said he: "They both believed in truth with a capital T." Then he solemnly advised, "A little life advice: if you ever run into someone who believes in truth with a capital T, you run as far and as fast as you possibly can away from that person, because that kind of person could kill you."

Relativistic Tolerance or Transcendent Toleration?

By the way, the whole basis of the modern, secular ideal of "tolerance" (on full display in multiculturalism) is that people who believe in absolute truth will kill you, or at least discriminate against and oppress you, and the only way that we can live amongst one another in peace and freedom is to deny that there is such a thing as absolute truth. But this kind of tolerance is not real toleration and cannot sustain real toleration. This kind of tolerance cannot have its root in the absolute, unchangeable law of God, because it denies the very existence of absolute universal truth and a transcendent deity while at the same time asserting, by sheer whim, a universal human right.

Thus, this kind of tolerance is completely unreliable and unstable. It requires everyone to relinquish claims to truth in the interests of liberty, and it gives not a thought to what happens if someone raises a question about the truth of the assertion that all people and views ought to be tolerated. Why? Multiculturalism has no sufficient answer. It has simply retained a moral impulse from a view of reality that it has rejected (orthodox Christianity) without anything to justify it but an inerasable moral sense that God has planted in every human heart.

A Gospel Opportunity to Engage the Culture

This is an area where orthodox Christians, precisely because we believe in absolute truth, have a decided apologetic advantage and opportunity in a relativistic culture. Real toleration was invented by Christians, and it was based on the doctrine of the image of God in man and on the doctrine of monergistic conversion. The concept and experience of freedom of religion, for instance, that we take for granted and enjoy today is the legacy of Reformation-era Christianity, the Puritan struggles in England, and the free church struggles here in colonial America (especially among Baptists and Presbyterians who were often hindered from the free exercise of religion by their Episcopalian neighbors in the South and Mid-Atlantic colonies and by their Congregationalist neighbors in New England).

The toleration they fostered was based on transcendent truth, not its rejection. Religious freedom, they argued, was based on absolute truth, not its denial. Thus, religious freedom was an inalienable right because it wasn't bestowed by social convention but by the Creator himself. Eugene Genovese describes this in his brilliant 1992 Massey Lectures at Harvard.[7] He comments that religious minorities in nineteenth-century America, particularly Catholics and Jews, often reported feeling more accepted and better treated in societies dominated by conservative, Protestant Christians than they did among liberal progressives. Now, you might not have expected that. So how did conservative Protestants manage to tolerate, welcome, and show neighbor-love to people with whom they strenuously disagreed? It was by their conviction of absolute truth. God has made people in his image, and thus we must treat them with dignity and respect commensurate to their nature. Conversion can never be coerced, because it is the work of God the Spirit. Therefore, forced conversion is illegitimate, and toleration of errant views that do not threaten the general welfare is necessary.

Genovese humorously characterizes the foundations of tolerance according to liberal progressives this way: "You worship God in *your* way, and I'll worship Him in *mine*," and we can all get along because religion is just opinion anyway, whether it's mine or yours, and who is right really doesn't matter much anyway. But, strangely, this *laissez-faire* approach did not produce as warm a welcome for religious minorities for some reasons that I won't go into here. Meanwhile, Genovese says that the basis of toleration in conservative Protestant communities was, "You worship God in *your* way, and I'll worship Him in *His*." In other words, they were not about to build a basis for mutual life and toleration on the denial of absolute truth or on the admission that the truth was relative, but rather on the very foundation of transcendent truth. They were going to respect the image of God in people who differed with them about things that matter eternally. It is that kind of commitment to truth that we need to foster among Christians and in the churches today as they engage with a relativistic culture.

Summary

The whole point of all this—mentioning the "deeds not creeds" and "people over truth" mind-sets and quoting the rabbi's confused antipathy for theology—is to illustrate that the attitude of suspicion toward theology, while internally inconsistent, is widespread in our culture and even evident in our churches. There is a plausibility to all this in the ears and hearts of the occupants of our time, and even in our congregations.

Emerging Problems with Systematic Theology?

Let's move on more particularly to the matter of systematic theology. Like propositional truth—doctrine and theology in general—there is a widespread misgiving about and rejection of systematic theology. The emergents typify this, but they are far from alone. In his widely referenced (and very encouraging) book, *Young, Restless, and Reformed*, Collin Hansen quotes Scot McKnight on systematic theology:

> The emerging movement tends to be suspicious of systematic theology. Why? Not because we don't read systematics, but because the diversity of theologies alarms us. No genuine consensus has been achieved, God didn't reveal a systematic theology, but a storied narrative; and no language is capable of capturing the Absolute Truth who alone is God.[8]

Note in particular two parts of McKnight's argument. ST is held in suspicion because (1) God didn't reveal a systematic theology but a storied narrative, and (2) language is not capable of capturing the "Absolute Truth" of God. Notice again here the emphasis that truth is a person more than or rather than a proposition about a person.

REJOINDER

That two-part argument is fallacious and unbiblical. It is fallacious in that it asserts that the Bible is a storied narrative. The Bible is not a storied narrative. It is God's one Word to his people coming to us in a library, a collection of sixty-six separate items written in three languages, composed and collected over about fifteen hundred years, containing a stunning variety of literary types: written history, personal memoirs, sermons, letters, hymns, prayers, propositions both moral and theological, creeds, love poetry, philosophy, family trees, visions, tales, statistics, public laws, rubrics, rituals, inventories, individual and corporate commands and directives, and more.

It is not a storied narrative. Indeed, we have to put the meta-narrative, the big picture, together, and to do that we not only derive it from specific passages that rehearse the overarching story, but we also do it with biblical (redemptive-historical) and systematic (summarizing topical) theology. So he is just wrong about that. The minute you admit that it is God's one Word—one message coming to us in diverse form—and reckon adequately with that reality, you immediately see why systematic theology is both necessary and unavoidable.

By the way, when you hear someone touting story and narrative over doctrine and propositions because, they opine, "this generation prefers narrative to proposition," then remember two things. First, this is not the first generation in history to like stories. People have always liked stories. Do you think that when seventeenth- or eighteenth-century dads tucked their children in bed at night that their bairns begged, "No stories tonight, Dad; we'd like syllogisms instead"? "Logic please, Pop." "No scary tales, sir. Restate those propositions one more time." Heavens, no! We've always liked stories. Second, oral cultures often used stories to convey doctrinal, moral, and political propositions. The story conveys the truth of the propositions but in a different, interesting, sometimes surprising and delightful way. The use of a story does not entail a rejection of or prejudice against propositions. One can even see this principle at work in Mosaic case law, in which legal propositions are illustrated by concrete (but not exhaustive) instances—stories—of its application. So the assertion that "we can't do doctrine anymore because this generation likes stories" is bogus.

Here is the second part of the problem with McKnight's argument: the objection that language is not capable of conveying absolute truth about God is not an objection that you can find in the pages of Scripture. It comes from an alien philosophical origin. That doesn't mean that Scripture does not assert (it most certainly does) the omnipotence of God and the infinity of God, and the eternality of God, and the other-ness of God. But you don't get into Genesis 2 and find Adam fretting over whether he can have a conversation with God, or if he can understand the command that God has given him. He clearly can. And even after the fall, God talks to us, and he assumes that we can understand him.

No, the objection that language is not capable of conveying absolute truth is not an angst derived from the pages of Scripture; it comes from an alien philosophical mind-set manifested in both medieval nominalism and post-Kantian philosophy. Both the apostle Paul and the apostle John were ready to expel people from the church over language! There were patterns of sound words that were to be kept, held fast to, and treasured. There were doctrines expressed in propositions that were nonnegotiable. "By this you know the Spirit of God: every spirit that confesses that Jesus Christ has come in the flesh is from God, and every spirit that does not confess Jesus is not from God. This is the spirit of the antichrist, which you heard was coming and now is in the world already" (1 John 4:2–3).[9] So affirming the humanity of Jesus and that he came "in the flesh" was not a negotiable in the apostle John's category of teaching.

Nor does this lead us down the path of denying that human language about and knowledge of God is analogical, rather than either univocal or equivocal. The Protestant Scholastic theologians of the post-Reformation era, who are so often maligned, rightly stressed the difference between archetypal and ectypal theology. We cannot know like God knows (archetypal), but we can know as God wants and allows and helps us to know (ectypal). McKnight's language objection is not a protest against our pretensions to archetypal knowledge of God, which we do not make, but against the very possibility of a reliable ectypal knowledge, which we acknowledge on biblical grounds.

Systematic or Biblical Theology?

Carl Trueman has recently commented:

> The wedge that has been consciously driven between systematic theology and biblical theology over recent decades in influential circles is starting to bear very bad fruit. Exclusive emphasis on the Bible as storytelling has combined with a trendy cultural impatience both with the past and with the very idea of systematic theology, and this has provided fertile soil for the reception of the kind of ideas promoted by the scripture revisionists [those who are denying or undermining biblical inerrancy].[10]

I need to say clearly that I love biblical theology. Biblical theology, the study of special revelation from the standpoint of the history of redemption, is an important and helpful theological discipline. I have been teaching biblical theology at the graduate level for almost twenty years. It is my favorite course to teach. So nothing I am about to say should lead you to think otherwise.

Biblical theology and systematic theology, done rightly, are friends. They need each other. They complement one another. And there are many outstanding evangelical scholars who recognize and model an appreciation of this in their professional ministry. One thinks of the late Geerhardus Vos and the late John Murray, both of whom had a healthy respect for each of these theological disciplines. In our own time, Dick Gaffin, Palmer Robertson, Sinclair Ferguson, Don Carson, and others too many to mention have modeled a healthy appropriation and integration of the two. The outstanding Old Testament scholar Bruce Waltke, whose writings have been such a help to me over the years (and whose massive *Old Testament Theology* is well worth your reading), affirms this kind of cooperative view of these disciplines:

> In my view the church is best served when biblical theologians work in conversation with orthodox systematic theology regarding the Bible (bibliology) as the foundation and boundary in matters deciding the basis, goal, and methodology for biblical theology. . . . Through this interpenetration of the two disciplines, we will be better able to present the theological power and religious appeal of biblical concepts.[11]

Amen to that!

A Skewed Description of Systematic Theology

Waltke, however, goes on to describe the two disciplines as follows:

> Systematic (dogmatic) theologians present the Christian message to the contemporary world. They draw the impetus for organizing this message from outside the Old Testament. John Calvin, in his justly famous *Institutes of the Christian Religion*, organized his material according to the four divisions of the Apostles' Creed. Philip Melanchthon organized his theology according to one book of the Bible, Romans. Since the seventeenth century, theologians typically employed philosophical categories derived from Greek thought, like bibliology (the study of the Bible), harmartiology (the study of sin), pneumatology (the study of the Spirit), and so on.
>
> Biblical theologians differ from dogmaticians in three ways. First, biblical theologians primarily think as exegetes, not as logicians. Second, they derive their organizational principle from the biblical blocks of writings themselves rather than from factors external to the text. Third, their thinking is diachronic—that is, they track the development of theological themes in various blocks of writings. Systematic theologians think more synchronic-

ally—that is, they invest their energies on the church's doctrines,
not on the development of religious ideas within the Bible.[12]

Well, yes and no, and because of the admixture of true and false
here, this description is, in the end, not helpful. And that's my reason for referencing it. Waltke is not trying to devalue ST, but he ends
up doing so definitionally.

Yes, it is true that biblical theology works diachronically (it
studies the text of Scripture from the standpoint of the historical
progress of redemption), and ST studies the Bible synchronically
(that's good—we need to do both); that is, it asks, "What does the
whole Bible teach about this topic or that topic?" But three things
need to be noted about this. (1) ST studies the Bible synchronically,
meaning that it coordinates and synthesizes the whole witness of
Scripture on the various topics it addresses but takes into account
what biblical theology has gleaned from its diachronic study.
(2) The Bible itself provides examples of this kind of synchronic
or topical study, as we shall soon see. (3) Pastors do this kind of
synchronic ST work all the time as well, and it is important and
essential that they do.

When a congregation member comes up to you and says,
"Pastor, tell me, what does the Bible say about angels?" he doesn't
want a storied narrative. He wants a brief, biblical summarization
that takes into account the shape of all the teaching of Scripture on
that particular topic. That's what systematic theology does. You
do it all the time as a pastor. So when your congregation member
asks you, "Pastor, what does the Bible teach about the assurance of
salvation?" or "Pastor, what does the Bible say about what happens
to us when we die?" your answer is indebted to systematic theology,
and you are doing systematic theology when you ask and answer
those kinds of questions. Systematic theology answers the question, what does the whole Bible teach us today about *X*? Doctrine
is what the whole Bible teaches about a particular topic; systematic

theology is the attempt to look carefully at what the Bible teaches about those doctrines, to summarize them helpfully, and to relate them to one another in a way that does justice to the teaching of the whole Bible.

Furthermore, the idea that biblical theologians think as exegetes while systematic theologians think as logicians is, well, laughable. But it is a sadly common charge, though I know of no systematic theologian at any major reformed and evangelical seminary who would describe or practice his work, in relation to biblical theology, this way. After all, even Karl Barth said, "Theology is exegesis!" Or, as John Murray better said, "Systematic theology is tied to exegesis."

Finally, the idea that ST is based on factors external to the text while biblical theology is organized by factors within the writings themselves is also an inadequate and misleading characterization. We all have to deal with the hermeneutical spiral, whether we are exegetes, biblical theologians, or systematicians. And it is impossible for orthodox biblical theologians to set aside all their systematic commitments when plying their trade. In the end, good systematic theologians are just as interested as good biblical theologians are to read the text respectfully, to listen to the text carefully, to make sure they are not importing alien questions and categories into their exegesis, and to let the truth of the Word shape their theology rather than allowing pre-understandings to dominate the text. We all want to sit at the feet of the Master, and the only way we can do that is to sit under the judgment of (and not over) his Word, submitting everything, especially our theology, to the searching truth of the Scriptures.

Again, the point of interacting with the Waltke quote is that even in the most sympathetic of evangelical and Reformed circles we can find the project of ST being misconstrued and even undermined. And far more flagrant examples would be easy to cite. One thinks of the work of John Franke, for instance.

Conclusion

The conclusion is that doctrine might be held in suspicion, but it is unavoidable and important. It is not hard to find examples in the church and world today of an anti-doctrinal, anti-theological, anti-ST mind-set. What I am going to argue, contra this outlook, is that it is impossible for us to avoid theology and doctrine. Everyone is a theologian, and everyone has doctrine. The issues are: (1) Are you a good theologian or a bad theologian? (2) Is your doctrine right or wrong? (3) Are you biblically faithful in the way you are articulating your theology? No one can avoid theology and doctrine. In fact, ST is actually unavoidable and necessary. You cannot *not* do systematic theology. Indeed, the Bible itself provides us with examples of systematic theology.

So, if somebody tells you that they don't believe in ST, watch out! They are about to slide their ST under the door without you looking. You can't *not* do ST, and ST done biblically is good for us. It brings glory to God. It informs our Christian living. And the Bible itself provides us with examples of it.

2) Necessary and Unavoidable

Scripture shows that truth, doctrine, and theology are necessary and important for the Christian life and that systematic theology is, in fact, unavoidable. There is a pan-biblical emphasis on the importance of truth for the Christian life, the necessity of doctrine for our walking with God, and if we are careful to observe how the Bible makes these points, we will also see why ST is necessary and unavoidable—and not something that you'd want to avoid anyway, but something that we all want to do well. Take, for instance, the following six passages in the Gospels and in Paul's Pastoral Epistles.

Right in the middle of the High Priestly Prayer, Jesus makes clear God's truth for our joy and growth in holiness. In this context, truth is not faithfulness or a person but is explicitly associated with God's Word:

But now I am coming to you, and these things I speak in the world, that they may have my joy fulfilled in themselves. I have given them your word, and the world has hated them because they are not of the world, just as I am not of the world. I do not ask that you take them out of the world, but that you keep them from the evil one. They are not of the world, just as I am not of the world. Sanctify them in the truth; your word is truth. (John 17:13–17)

In the Great Commission itself, Jesus tells his disciples to teach the church not simply to believe his instruction and to teach all of it but to teach it with a view to his people living out the truth—his truth:

Jesus came and said to them, "All authority in heaven and on earth has been given to me. Go therefore and make disciples of all nations, baptizing them in the name of the Father and of the Son and of the Holy Spirit, teaching them to observe all that I have commanded you. And behold, I am with you always, to the end of the age." (Matt. 28:18–20)

In a seminal passage for understanding the apostolic theology of ministry, Paul tells Timothy, negatively, not to allow people to teach or listen to bad theology and, positively, that good theology aims for true, heart-rooted, lived-out, gospel love in believers:

As I urged you when I was going to Macedonia, remain at Ephesus that you may charge certain persons not to teach any different doctrine, nor to devote themselves to myths and endless genealogies, which promote speculations rather than the steward-ship from God that is by faith. The aim of our charge is love that issues from a pure heart and a good conscience and a sincere faith. (1 Tim. 1:3–5)

In an important passage on the law in the Christian life, Paul makes clear that doctrine and ethics are inseparably connected.

Indeed, he says that the gospel itself and doctrine are inextricably tied to a certain kind of life:

> Now we know that the law is good, if one uses it lawfully, understanding this, that the law is not laid down for the just but for the lawless and disobedient, for the ungodly and sinners, for the unholy and profane, for those who strike their fathers and mothers, for murderers, the sexually immoral, men who practice homosexuality, enslavers, liars, perjurers, and whatever else is contrary to sound doctrine, in accordance with the glory of the gospel of the blessed God with which I have been entrusted. (1 Tim. 1:8–11)

Paul shows not only a concern with orthodox doctrine but that he even cares about retaining the pattern of words of Jesus' teaching, and he articulates a major principle of his theology—doctrine is unto godliness:

> Teach and urge these things. If anyone teaches a different doctrine and does not agree with the sound words of our Lord Jesus Christ and the teaching that accords with godliness, he is puffed up with conceit and understands nothing. (1 Tim. 6:2–4)

Again Paul connects truth and godliness, because knowledge of truth is vital to godliness:

> Paul, a servant of God and an apostle of Jesus Christ, for the sake of the faith of God's elect and their knowledge of the truth, which accords with godliness. (Titus 1:1)

Those six passages show the legitimacy of the categories and importance of truth, doctrine, and theology. Let's take some time to walk through the passages and see how. We could go to literally dozens of examples in the Bible, but for now let's confine ourselves to these six.

Truth Is for Joy and Growth

The first passage is a portion of the High Priestly Prayer of John 17, in which Jesus utters the immortal petition of verse 17: "Sanctify them in the truth; your word is truth" (v. 17). In this passage we find the Lord Jesus Christ praying to his heavenly Father in anticipation of his ascension, on the other side of his crucifixion and death and burial and resurrection. He says, "I am coming to you" so that they might "have my joy fulfilled in themselves." He is praying specifically that his disciples would understand that he is leaving them and going to the Father, and that they would be built up in the truth of the Word of the Father that he had been speaking to them, so that *his joy* would be fulfilled *in them*. Jesus is saying that truth is for joy. Doctrine is for delight, the Lord Jesus says. If you denigrate doctrine, you denigrate what Jesus says is necessary for joy. You are a killjoy if you are against doctrine, because the Lord Jesus says truth is for joy.

But Jesus doesn't stop there. He goes on to say that truth is for holiness, for growth in godliness, for sanctification. Notice again what he prays: "Sanctify them in the truth; your word is truth." It is God's Word that is going to set them apart from the world. He wants them to be in the world but not of it, and that is going to happen by the Word being in them, by the Word dwelling in them richly and making them holy. He prays, in effect: "Lord, I'm not asking that you would take them out of the world; I'm praying that you would *put your word in them.*"

Do you hear the echoes of that in Romans 12:1–2, where the apostle Paul says, "Do not be conformed to this world, but be transformed by the renewal of your mind"? And what are our minds renewed according to? God's Word, his truth! We are in the world, but the *Word* is in us, and therefore the world does not take us captive. The Word sets us free. So we see that Jesus says that truth is for our joy, our growth, our holiness, our godliness.

Truth Is to Be Lived

Second, in Matthew 28:18–20, Jesus says to his disciples, just a few weeks after he had prayed the prayer in the upper room, "All authority in heaven and on earth has been given to me. Go therefore and make disciples of all nations, baptizing them in the name of the Father and of the Son and of the Holy Spirit, *teaching them to observe all that I have commanded you.* And behold, I am with you always, to the end of the age." That is truly fascinating, don't you think? Jesus isn't telling them to go and teach a very simple gospel outline. Rather, disciples are made as they are taught to live everything that Jesus taught. He says, "Here's what I want you to do. I want you to go and make disciples of all the nations, and I want you to teach them a very simple gospel outline. You know, just stick to the ABCs. Nothing too complex." No, that's not what Jesus says. He says, "Here's how you make a disciple, you teach him everything that I ever taught you, and not just to know it and believe it, but to live it. Teach them to live my truth. I want you to teach them everything that I ever taught you, and I want you to teach them to live it out."

The point is simple. Disciples are made by sitting under apostolic (biblical) teaching that conveys all the truth that Jesus taught his disciples with a view to that truth being lived out. Doctrine is to be practiced, lived, obeyed, and observed.

Errant Doctrine Destroys, True Doctrine
Leads to Love

Third, notice Paul's opening emphasis to Timothy in 1 Timothy 1:3–5, and as you do, think about this: if you were sitting down to write the all-time best-selling book on pastoral theology, how would you start it? I bet you wouldn't start the way the apostle Paul starts. The first directive out of his mouth in his all-time best seller on pastoral theology is, "As I urged you when I was going to Macedonia, remain at Ephesus so that you may charge certain persons not to teach any different doctrine." Stunning, isn't it? Pastoral theology, point one: "Timothy: tell them not to teach bad theology. Here's job one: make sure that false teachers are not persuading the people of God with errant views, opinions, and teachings that will not lead to godliness but rather to vain speculation and division and ruin and destruction." Paul's first point to Timothy is that bad theology will ruin people's lives.

This leads right to Paul's second point: hindering false teaching and fostering sound doctrine is so important because sound theology is, by the work of God's Spirit, productive of love. Thus, the true, faithful, and sound theology that we are teaching, the goal of our instruction, has love in view—love from a pure heart and a good conscience and sincere faith. Good theology is designed by God to work its way deep into our hearts and bones by the Holy Spirit, and it has in view the production of a life of love.

By the way, this is just one reason I treasure the brothers from Sovereign Grace (C. J., Josh, Bob, Jeff, et al.) so much. They get this. Truth is for joy, delight, and love. They are happy Calvinists. What a concept! Loving the truth and loving people so much that they want them to know the truth and live in love, and they're happy about it all. This is great!

Life and Doctrine Are Inseparable

Fourth, in 1 Timothy 1:8–11, Paul once again shows the connection between truth and life, doctrine and ethics. Having summarized the moral law using an abbreviated form of the Ten Commandments, he says that ethical violations of those commands are "contrary to sound doctrine," and he doesn't just mean ethical teaching. For Paul, here and everywhere (as with Jesus), people do what they really believe. Doctrine is linked to behavior.

Do you see what Paul is saying? He is saying that life—ethics, morality, behavior, practice—is inextricably tied to doctrine. Immorality, evil deeds, and sinful behavior find their root in the rejection of true teaching. They both evidence and lead to a rejection of true teaching. Paul not only says that ungodly behavior is contrary to sound doctrine, but he indicates that it is out of accord with the gospel. The true life that is to be lived by the believer is to be in accordance with the glorious gospel of the blessed God. So not only sound doctrine but the gospel itself is inextricably connected to the living of the Christian life.

Good Doctrine Promotes Godliness

Fifth, in 1 Timothy 6:2–4, Paul makes clear that there are immovable norms for doctrinal orthodoxy. There is right doctrine over against which "different doctrine" can be distinguished; there are "the sound words of our Lord Jesus Christ" with which false teaching can be identified and contrasted; and there is an invariable product of true doctrine that has been applied rightly in the lives of disciples—"the teaching that accords with godliness"— over against which the speculations of the false teachers issue forth in lives that disprove the truth of their teachings. Paul's use of the phrase "the sound words of our Lord Jesus Christ" indicates his confidence in the capacity of human language, though situated, to convey universally authoritative, understandable, applicable, and profitable truth. Then there is his beautiful statement that doctrine is unto godliness. The purpose of truth, doctrine, and theology, and the purpose of his doctrinal teaching, is the promotion of godliness.

The Pastoral Importance of Truth

Sixth, and finally, in Titus 1:1 Paul barely gets out of his salutation before he mentions the pastoral importance of truth. Servants of the Word minister so that faith and truth issue forth in the godliness of believers. Paul's apostolic service is "for the sake of the faith of God's elect and their knowledge of the truth, which accords with godliness." Notice again Paul's saying that knowledge of truth is vital to godliness. Why should that be a surprise? Jesus had already prayed, "Lord, sanctify them with truth. Your word is truth." Paul has just learned from Jesus that truth is unto godliness.

I love the way Donald Macleod, in his lectures on Philippians 2 and Christology, stresses this Pauline point:

> Paul uses the Christological teaching [in Philippians 2] precisely because of its relevance to the pastoral problems in the church at Philippi. That is enormously instructive, because it reminds us that theology does not exist in a vacuum. It exists in the interest of pastoralia [things pertaining to pastoral ministry]. It exists in order to be applied to the day-to-day problems of the Christian church. Every doctrine has its application. All scripture is profitable and all the doctrine is profitable. Similarly all the application must be based on doctrine. In both the Philippians example-passage and the Corinthian example-passage, Paul is dealing with what are surely comparative trivia, the problem of vain glory in a Christian congregation and the problem of failure of Christian liberality. As a Pastor one meets with these difficulties daily. They are standing problems. Yet Paul as he wrestles with both of them has recourse to the most massive theology. It's not only that you have the emphasis on the unity between theology and practice but you have the emphasis on the applicability of the profoundest theology to the most mundane and most common-place problems. Who would ever imagine that the response to the glory of the incarnation might be to give to the collection for the poor? Who might imagine that the application of the glories of New Testament Christology might be to stop our quarreling and our divisiveness in the Christian ekklesia? That is what Paul is doing here. He is telling them: You have these practical problems; the answer is theological; remember your theology and place your behaviour in the light of that theology. Place your little problems in the light of the most massive theology. We ourselves in our Christian callings are to be conscious of this. We must never leave our doctrine hanging in the air, nor hesitate to enforce the most elementary Christian obligations with the most sublime doctrines.[13]

Friends, in this anti-doctrinal/anti-theological age, I want to say this loudly and clearly: truth matters. Teaching matters. Doctrine matters. Doctrinal instruction matters. Theology is for life. Theology, William Perkins rightly said, "is the science of living blessedly ever after." William Ames truly said: "Theology is the doctrine or teaching of living to God." And yet we live in an anti-doctrinal/anti-theological age, and some are saying that we need to embrace the postmodern uncertainty about truth and the postmodern aversion to doctrine by embracing postmodern uncertainty and rejecting doctrine in favor of narrative and story.

Over against that I want to suggest that that is exactly the opposite of what we need to do. We need to meet this postmodern uncertainty, this postmodern aversion to truth and doctrine, by celebrating truth and doctrine and by unashamedly asserting and declaring theology. I want to urge that your preaching, which ought to be expositional, ought also to be robustly theological. We need to be joyfully and emphatically doctrinal and theological in our ministry. I don't mean that we ought to bring the vocabulary of the seminary into our pulpits (that's not what we need to do); but I do mean that we need to bring the substance of the Bible's theology into our preaching and bring our people into contact with it. We need to see the value of truth, doctrine, and theology, and we need to out-live and out-rejoice and out-die the critics of theology and doctrine.

Is Evangelicalism Neo-Erasmian?

I hear echoes of Erasmus in those who devalue doctrine in our day. One of the interesting things about the sixteenth-century debate between Luther and Erasmus over the freedom and bondage of the will is that Erasmus showed himself to be fundamentally indifferent toward doctrinal questions, not unlike many evangelicals of today. Erasmus held that matters of doctrine are relatively unimportant because, for him, Christianity was essentially morality, a life more than a doctrine. But doctrinal indifference endangers the gospel, which is emphatically not a set of ethical dictates, and turns Christianity into moralism. Luther, on the other hand, could not have disagreed more with Erasmus's views of "apostolic simplicity in faith and life." Luther was emphatically doctrinal and theological.

J. I. Packer and O. R. Johnston, in their outstanding introduction to Luther's *Bondage of the Will*, capture Luther's concern for doctrine superbly. In contrast to Erasmus, they say:

> Luther's attitude was very different. To him, Christianity was a matter of doctrine first and foremost, because true religion was first and foremost a matter of faith; and faith is correlative to truth. Faith is trust in God through Jesus Christ as He stands revealed in the gospel. Accordingly, "assertions"—doctrinal statements embodying the contents of the gospel—are fundamental to the Christian religion. Christianity was to Luther a dogmatic religion, or it was nothing. "Take away assertions, and you take away Christianity," he writes. "That would be denying all religion and piety in one breath." As Principal Watson emphasises, Luther's first concern, as theologian and reformer, was with doctrine. "I am not concerned with the life, but with doctrines," he declared. This, he held, was what distinguished him from reforming spirits of earlier days. "Others, who have lived before me have attacked the Pope's evil and scandalous life, but I have attacked his doctrine." Accordingly, Luther will have no truck with Erasmus' conception of an undogmatic Christianity, and the humanist's airy indifference to matters of doctrine seemed to him essentially un-Christian as anything well could be. For the Christian "assertions" were no mere hit-or-miss rationalisations of religious experience; what they contained was the revealed truth of God, recorded in Scripture for the Church's instruction and sealed upon the believer's heart by the saving enlightenment of the Holy Spirit. [Luther says] "The Holy Spirit is no Sceptic, and the things He has written in our hearts are not doubts or opinions, but assertions—surer and more certain than sense of life itself."[14]

But What about Systematic Theology?

Having said all this, we have yet to make our argument for the legitimacy, necessity, importance, and unavoidability of ST. The fact of the matter is that we find systematic theology being done in the Bible. Consider these very important passages.

The Locus Classicus of Biblical Theology (and ST)

> He said to them, "O foolish ones, and slow of heart to believe all that the prophets have spoken! Was it not necessary that the Christ should suffer these things and enter into his glory?" And beginning with Moses and all the Prophets, he interpreted to them in all the Scriptures the things concerning himself. (Luke 24:25–27)

This is the famous passage from the road to Emmaus. It is also one of the favorite passages on which to base the discipline of biblical theology, especially when wanting to stress a Christ-centered interpretation of redemptive history, and it is true and legitimate to deduce it from this passage. But think for a moment: what does that deduction entail? To ask the question another way, what did Jesus show these forlorn disciples from all the Scriptures? He showed them not the storied narrative of redemptive history, but himself. The study is personal, topical, and systematic—not, in the first instance, historical. The focus is the person and work of Christ. The disciples were able to grasp the Christ-centeredness of redemptive history because of the Christological focus of his exposition and interpretation. As Geldenhuys says, "And then the Saviour, who knows the Word of God perfectly, because of His intimate union with the Spirit who is its Primary Author, expounded to them in broad outline all the Scriptures that referred to Him, from the first books of the Old Testament and right through to the end."[15]

Luke tells us specifically that the topical focus was the humiliation and exaltation of the Messiah in passages that showed that the

Messiah must suffer before his glory came: "Was it not necessary that the Christ should suffer these things and enter into his glory?" It is interesting that great twentieth-century Dutch dogmatician Herman Bavinck, like some of the unjustly maligned Protestant Scholastics before him, structured his systematic presentation of Christology around these twin themes.

But don't miss the point. In Luke 24:27, we see Jesus doing systematic theology about Jesus! Jesus is teaching a course in Christology from the whole Hebrew Bible, not merely answering what this genre or that writer emphasizes about him. No, he is looking at the big picture—the total witness of the Hebrew Bible to his person and work. And that, my friends, is systematic theology.

Apollos and Paul, Systematic Theologians

> When he arrived, he greatly helped those who through grace had believed, for he powerfully refuted the Jews in public, showing by the Scriptures that the Christ was Jesus. (Acts 18:27–28)
>
> And Paul went in, as was his custom, and on three Sabbath days he reasoned with them from the Scriptures, explaining and proving that it was necessary for the Christ to suffer and to rise from the dead, and saying, "This Jesus, whom I proclaim to you, is the Christ." (Acts 17:2–3)

Apollos and the apostle Paul did the same thing that Jesus did on the road to Emmaus. Apollos gave a robust defense of Christian Christology, showing from the whole Hebrew Bible the biblical basis of the Christian truth-claim that Jesus is the predicted Messiah. This is a systematic study of the messiahship of Jesus. As such, it is topical and synchronic rather than redemptive-historical, although it has huge ramifications for a redemptive-historical reading of the Bible.

Luke draws attention to the fact that polemics, the refutation of false teaching, is good for Christians: "He greatly helped those who through grace had believed, for he powerfully refuted the Jews in public." Have you ever thought that refutation of false doctrine encourages the brethren? Well, that's what Luke says. It strikes me as I think of it that the most enduring and edifying legacy of the early post-apostolic church is found in their polemics. When they were arguing against false teaching, they almost always got it right. When they were not, they were theologically hit-or-miss. But what I want you to see in the passage is that Apollos does the same thing that Jesus did in Luke 24. It's a systematic study of the Bible's teaching on the messiahship of Christ.

In Acts 17 Paul not only gives a defense of the identification of Jesus as Messiah, but even more he exactly duplicates what Luke recorded Jesus doing (Luke 24). He explained and proved "that it was necessary for the Christ to suffer and to rise from the dead." By the way, the early, post-apostolic church followed in the wake of Jesus, Paul, and Apollos in assembling their own *demonstratio evangelica*, or proof of the gospel, which became the title of one of Eusebius's books in the early fourth century from the Old Testament texts. While these Christologically organized collections of proof-texts for Christian truth claims could be sometimes morphed into redemptive-historical form, as in Irenaeus's *Demonstration of the Apostolic Preaching*, the organizational principle is strictly personal, topical, and Christological, and thus systematic. They studied what the whole Hebrew Bible taught them about the Messiah.

Further Biblical Testimony for the Practice of Systematic Theology

How are New Testament books organized and what does that say about ST? One does not simply have to rely on the testimony of exemplary tests to show the legitimacy of ST from the Bible. For instance, note the shape of many of the Pauline letters. They are not organized around redemptive history but around the loci of "doctrine" and "living" (theology/ethics and truth/practice). Think of the book of Romans (chaps. 1–11, doctrine; chaps. 12–16, ethics).

There is plenty of good redemptive-historical material in the first eleven chapters, but the overarching organizational principle of the book is not redemptive-historical but systematic.

The same could be said for Ephesians and Philippians. By the way, this pattern of doctrine then duty, or theology then ethics, or truth then life, found in some of Paul's letters is precisely the outline of dogmatic theology adopted by the members of the Westminster Assembly (1643–1649) in the Westminster Confession of Faith and catechisms. The Westminster Confession of Faith is structured with chapters 1 to 18 on doctrine and chapters 19 to 33 on the Christian life. The catechisms are shaped the same way. Consequently, the official confession statements of Presbyterians (later modified and used by Baptists and Congregationalists, as well) followed an explicitly Pauline organizing principle. This shows that it is possible to organize our study of systematic theology with sensitivity to the shape of Scripture.

Even the Gospels, which provide our main insight into the history of Christ's life and ministry, bear the marks of theological concerns, and these concerns contribute to the organization of the Gospels. If your main goal was to write a biography of Jesus, would you leave out all but about the last five years of his life and spend about a quarter of your words on the week of his crucifixion? That's what Matthew does, because he is zeroing in on the atoning work of Christ (in chaps. 21–28) and that topical, systematic theological concern shapes the organization and proportion of his material. John's presentation is even more skewed. Almost half of his Gospel takes place during Passion Week; we find ourselves in the upper room by chapter 13. Atonement, the meaning and significance of the death of Christ, is a staggeringly important topical, systematic category for shaping organization and proportion.

The same could be said for the author of Hebrews. Topical considerations repeatedly influence his organization of material. Think of his focus on the divine sonship of Christ in Hebrews 1, or his exposition of the nature of true faith in Hebrews 11. The redemptive-historical aspect is there to be sure, but in the end a topical focus and a pastoral concern drive the shape of the material. That is good ST at work.

In case you are tempted to think that ST is only a New Testament phenomenon, we could just as easily show how theological, not just historical, considerations shaped the Chronicler's organization of 1 and 2 Chronicles and shaped the authors/editors of the other historical books (e.g., Kings and Samuel). Or we could point out how Genesis 3–11 functions to set forth a very definite doctrine of sin, preceding the grand redemptive narrative of Abraham. Theological considerations mark the organization of Scripture everywhere. To suggest that these same considerations can play no part in our organization of our study of the Bible is strange indeed, and literally unbiblical.

New Testament Citation Formulas

What do the citation formulas of the New Testament teach us about ST? The formulas of Old Testament citation used by New Testament authors also reveal their belief in the unity of Scripture, e.g., "It says," "Scripture says," "God says." B. B. Warfield wrote a brilliant article a century ago showing how these citation formulas indicate a high view of Scripture, and he is right—they do. But they also indicate that the divinely inspired New Testament authors thought that Scripture speaks as one. They could cite an author, a passage of Scripture, and because they believed that God himself was the ultimate author of Scripture, they could speak with confidence in the unity and harmony of Scripture's witness to the truth. In other words, the Bible itself gives us permission to say "the Bible says" without falling to the charge of dubious harmonization. The minute we say "the Bible says," we are unavoidably engaged in the work of ST because the text, as Waltke reminds us, is not fully topically arranged. If we are going to speak to a topic, the arranging has to be done. To be sure, it has to be done in conversation with exegetical theology, biblical theology, and even historical theology, but it requires us inescapably to do the work of ST.

So the notion that ST is an unbiblical intrusion upon our study of the Bible or an exercise in modernistic rationalism is actually quite easily dispelled by close attention to Scripture itself, which both does and requires ST.

Summary

ST works on the collection, summary, interrelation, and articulation of what the whole Bible teaches on the major topics that it addresses. ST is not an enemy of biblical theology but its benefactor. Biblical theology cannot provide the final assessment offered by ST, but it helps ST make that assessment. Wayne Grudem is crystal clear and helpful on this point:

> Systematic Theology . . . makes use of the material of biblical theology and often builds on the results of biblical theology. At some points, especially where great detail and care is needed in the development of doctrine, systematic theology will even use a biblical-theological method, analyzing the development of each doctrine through the historical development of Scripture. But the focus of systematic theology remains different: its focus is on the collection and then the summary of the teaching of all the biblical passages on a particular subject . . . . It [then] attempts to summarize the teaching of Scripture in a brief, understandable, and very carefully formulated statement.[16]

How helpful is ST? Extremely! It helps us to learn and teach what the whole Bible says. It helps us to overcome our wrong ideas and be corrected by Scripture. It helps us to assess new theological proposals. It helps us to grow as Christians. It helps us to distinguish between the "greater and lesser matters of the law." We'll conclude by further exploring the benefits of truth, doctrine, theology, and ST to the Christian life.

3) What Are Theology, Truth, and Doctrine Important For?

Let us consider four great passages and what they teach us about the application of theology. We have already argued that theology exists in the interest of *pastoralia*. We pastor the troubled heart the same way Jesus pastored his disciples. Jesus said, "Believe in God; believe also in me" (John 14:1). The way to calm the troubled breast is to know God. It is to know Christ as he is offered in the gospel. And that requires knowing truth, doctrine, and *theo*logy—truth about God, truth about Jesus Christ. And that means we must be *theo*logians in order to pastor and shepherd God's flock.[17]

God's Glory

Theology, doctrine, and truth are for God's glory. Paul makes this apparent in the stirring ending to the doctrinal portion of Romans:

> For God has consigned all to disobedience, that he may have mercy on all. Oh, the depth of the riches and wisdom and knowledge of God! How unsearchable are his judgments and how inscrutable his ways! "For who has known the mind of the Lord, or who has been his counselor?" "Or who has given a gift to him that he might be repaid?" For from him and through him and to him are all things. To him be glory forever. Amen. (Romans 11:32–36)

Have you ever wondered why Romans 11:33–36 follows verse 32a? What Paul says in verse 32a is stunningly grim: "For God has consigned all to disobedience." That is not a phrase, a truth, from which you are looking to say, "Can I get an Amen?" All three parts of the phrase confound us. *He consigned. All. To disobedience.* This is a deep thing, my friends. So how does Paul get from there to a doxology—to the great doxology? "Oh, the depth of the riches and wisdom and knowledge of God! How unsearchable are his judgments and how inscrutable his ways! . . . To him be the glory forever." He does it with the glorious phrase—"that he may have mercy on all."

Paul is saying that our sovereign God forced even the entrance of sin into the world and the preterition of the lost to serve the interests of the display of his glory in the display of his mercy and grace. Paul is saying that original sin, and all the actual sin that flows from it, and God's just condemnation of the wicked have been made (in the inscrutable wisdom of God) to show, demonstrate, display, evidence, and magnify his grace to the objects of his mercy. In other words, God has used spectacular sins and relentless judgment to display the glory of his grace. It takes our breath away.

So the mind-boggling, spine-tingling theology of Romans 9–11 is to serve the purposes of the display of God's glory. Doctrine is for God's glory. The doctrine of sovereignty serves the interests of his glory. The doctrine of sin serves the interests of his glory. The doctrines of election and preterition serve the interests of his glory. All doctrine is about his glory. All of it.

We memorize *The Children's Catechism* in the Presbyterian Church, and I had been working on it with my children for a while.

Q: Who made you?
A: God.
Q: What else did God make?
A: All things.
Q: Why did God make you and everything else?
A: For His own glory.

My son and daughter were out in the driveway one day. My son was playing on a California Chariot, which has been described as "a cross between a BMX bike, two skateboards, and a shopping cart" and as "a radically extreme scooter" (ah, Californians). He was hurtling down the pavement at impressive speeds and having a glorious time of it. He came over to me and asked, "Dad, why did God make California Chariots?"

My daughter immediately interrupted and said, "Jennings, God didn't make California Chariots! God made the people that made the California Chariots."

My son rolled his eyes, obviously thinking, "Thank you for that nuance and clarification on God's instrumental usage of means in the workings of his providence, Sis," and he turned right back to me and said, "Dad, why did God make California Chariots?"

I said, "I don't know, Jennings. I guess because he wanted little guys like you to have fun."

He said, "No, Dad. It was for his own glory!"

Well, he was right. And doctrine is one of the "all things" that God made for his own glory. Doctrine is for God's glory.

Assurance

Theology, doctrine, and truth are for our assurance. Nobody has ever made that point better than Jesus:

> No longer do I call you servants, for the servant does not know what his master is doing; but I have called you friends, for all that I have heard from my Father I have made known to you. You did not choose me, but I chose you and appointed you that you should go and bear fruit and that your fruit should abide, so that whatever you ask the Father in my name, he may give it to you. (John 15:15–16)

"You did not choose me, but I chose you" (v. 16), Jesus says in the upper room. He is going to die in a matter of hours for the sins of the world, and he is teaching them about election. Why was it so important for Jesus to teach his disciples about election here, that he had chosen them rather than them choosing him? It was important because, as Matthew tells us, they were all going to abandon him that night (Matt. 26:31). Not just Judas, but all of them. If they were going to have one shred of assurance left, it would not be based on the fact that they had chosen him or followed him or remained faithful to him, because everything about their actions that night and the next day would scream into their hearts and consciences that they had no part of him. That is why they had to hear the Master say, "Friend, I knew everything in you, I knew all you'd ever done and all you'd ever do, and I chose you anyway. I chose you and nothing can take you away from me." The doctrine of election is for assurance. Doctrine is for assurance.

Marriage

Theology, doctrine, and truth are for marriage. Paul gloriously brings that point home:

> Husbands, love your wives, as Christ loved the church and gave himself up for her, that he might sanctify her, having cleansed her by the washing of water with the word, so that he might present the church to himself in splendor, without spot or wrinkle or any such thing, that she might be holy and without blemish. In the same way husbands should love their wives as their own bodies. He who loves his wife loves himself. (Eph. 5:25–28)

The doctrine of the atoning work of our Lord Jesus Christ is at the heart of our salvation, and it is first and foremost a testimony to the unique, unrepeated, and unrepeatable work of the Lord Jesus Christ. It is a work he did for us, in our place, on our behalf, and we made and make absolutely no contribution to it. We performed and perform no part of it. It is totally outside of us. It is objective to us. We contributed nothing to it, though we benefit everything from it.

But it is interesting that Paul points to the atoning work of Christ and from it draws ethical obligations for us. We notice it especially in Ephesians 5:25: "Husbands, love your wives, as Christ loved the church and gave himself up for her." Paul is saying, "Husbands, every time you hear John Piper or R. C. Sproul or Al Mohler preaching on the atoning work of Christ, you first give glory to Christ, who paid for all your sins through the shedding of his blood. But the next thing you are to do is look up at your Lord Jesus and learn how to love your wife." You are to love your wife in light of the doctrine of the atonement. The atonement informs your love for your wife. You might say to me, "But she has broken my heart." But did not the church break her Lord's heart? And he loved her unto death. You love your wife like Christ loved the church in his giving up of himself for her in his atoning death. That's how you love her. The doctrine of atonement informs how a Christian husband conducts himself in marriage. Doctrine is for marriage.

Joy

Truth, theology, and doctrine are for joy. Again it is Paul who impresses this point upon our souls:

> Finally, my brothers, rejoice in the Lord. To write the same things to you is no trouble to me and is safe for you. Look out for the dogs, look out for the evildoers, look out for those who mutilate the flesh. For we are the circumcision, who worship by the Spirit of God and glory in Christ Jesus and put no confidence in the flesh—though I myself have reason for confidence in the flesh also. If anyone else thinks he has reason for confidence in the flesh, I have more: circumcised on the eighth day, of the people of Israel, of the tribe of Benjamin, a Hebrew of Hebrews; as to the law, a Pharisee; as to zeal, a persecutor of the church; as to righteousness under the law, blameless. But whatever gain I had, I counted as loss for the sake of Christ. Indeed, I count everything as loss because of the surpassing worth of knowing Christ Jesus my Lord. For his sake I have suffered the loss of all things and count them as rubbish, in order that I may gain Christ and be found in him, not having a righteousness of my own that comes from the law, but that which comes through faith in Christ, the righteousness from God that depends on faith—that I may know him and the power of his resurrection, and may share his sufferings, becoming like him in his death, that by any means possible I may attain the resurrection from the dead. (Phil. 3:1–11)

Paul opens this chapter in a fascinating way: "Finally, my brothers, rejoice in the Lord." After saying "Finally, my brothers . . . " Paul goes on for two more chapters. Some of you preachers are saying to yourselves, "I recognize this pattern! I've begun my conclusion, and then fifteen minutes and four points later, I'm finally getting to it." Commentators note that Paul gives his usual closing commendations at the end of Philippians 2 rather than at the end of the epistle, and then he launches into this supreme doctrinal exposition in chapter 3. What is going on here? "Rejoice in the Lord," and then doctrine. It seems so disconnected that liberal critics say that Philippians 3:1b–11 must have been written by somebody other than Paul. *Au contraire!*

But what is the connection between 3:1a and what follows? The short answer is this: joy-producing truth. Paul's great message in 1b–11 is to glory in Christ Jesus and put no confidence in the flesh, because nothing compares to Jesus and what he alone can give. Everything that Paul has given up in the flesh, every prized religious pedigree that he can boast of, he has counted as loss and rubbish, because none of it even remotely compares to the surpassing worth of knowing the Messiah. Through Jesus, his Lord, Paul knows and experiences the benefits of justification, sanctification, and glorification. The whole passage is a glorious doctrinal-experiential meditation on Christ and his benefits, and it brings Paul joy. He treasures Christ and contemplates the truth about him, the truth about his supremacy and his gifts. Paul bursts into rejoicing, and he wants the Philippians, and you and me, to do so as well. Christology—union with Christ, saving faith, justification, sanctification, and glorification—lead Paul to joy, because doctrine is for joy. That's why we say that the anti-doctrinists are killjoys.

Conclusion

My brothers in the ministry, don't starve your sheep; don't rob your sheep of the enjoyment of God's glory, assurance, and joy. They need truth, theology, and doctrine for God's glory, for their assurance, for the Christian life, for marriage, and for joy. You need to preach that truth because truth matters. Doctrine matters. Theology is for life. Good, biblical, systematic theology is not an encumbrance to the Christian life but a blessed and necessary aid. If you are a faithful pastor, you are a good systematic theologian. Study to show yourself approved. Live out your doctrine before the flock and the watching world, and teach it. When the detractors of doctrine come, then by the grace of the Holy Spirit out-study, out-teach, and out-pastor them. Out-live them, out-love them, out-rejoice them, out-suffer them, and out-die them.

CHAPTER 2

BEARING THE IMAGE

Thabiti Anyabwile

Our entire outlook on the world is so misplaced, wrongheaded, and inadequate that we need to either change it now or commit ourselves to the closest mental health facility. The problem is this: most of us operate with some working idea of race that is foundational to our worldview. But believing in race is like believing in unicorns, because neither race nor unicorns exist in reality.

I want to convince you that we have been looking at the world with a completely unbiblical set of assumptions. I want to convince you that we have organized our identities and lives on those assumptions and that we are in urgent need of acquiring a biblical set of assumptions that will shape not only our personal identities but also how we do ministry in the local church. We want to consider four ways in which we are unified that should shape how we think of one another: (1) unity in Adam; (2) unity in Christ; (3) unity in the church; and (4) unity in glory around the throne.

You might think of this as a theological baseball game. Our unity in Adam is akin to first base. First base is the most difficult base to reach, but you can't reach any of the other bases unless you have reached first base. So we'll spend a bit of time working on unity in Adam. Second base is our unity in Christ. In baseball, second base is, essentially, scoring position. A well-hit single with a runner on second will bring the runner home from there. In this life, while we await glory, unity in Christ is second base, the position from which to score. Third base is unity in the church. It is the closest base to home—necessary, exciting, full of anticipation—but it's not home yet. Home plate is the destiny for which we play the game. It's the promised eternity of loving, satisfying, joyous face-to-face fellowship with God our Father and Jesus our Savior, the Lamb of God who ransomed us with his own blood.

First Base: Unity in Adam

In getting to first base I want to convince you from the Scripture with the Spirit's blessing that what we call "race" does not, in fact, exist. Having convinced you of that, hopefully, I want to then enroll you in a personal and corporate campaign to (a) be rid of the very framework of race, (b) more fully adopt a new identity, and (c) teach others to do so as well. Typically, when we talk about our solidarity with Adam, we discuss our participation in Adam's sin. Adam—our federal head—fell into sin in Genesis 3 and plunged all of humanity and creation into sin with him. So we all share in Adam's sin.

But there are two other ways we have solidarity with Adam that precede Genesis 3 and also survive the fall in that chapter. First, there is a biological or genealogical solidarity with our first parents. Adam and Eve are the father and mother of all living people. Second, like Adam, God made us all in his image and likeness. We are image bearers with Adam.

The Bible and Race

I take it that these matters are obvious to most of us, but I want to briefly trace them in Scripture and then meditate on some implications of these truths that might not be so obvious. We start in Genesis 1:26–27:

> Then God said, "Let us make man in our image, after our likeness. And let them have dominion over the fish of the sea and over the birds of the heavens and over the livestock and over all the earth and over every creeping thing that creeps on the earth." So God created man in his own image, in the image of God he created him; male and female he created them.[1]

God announced on the sixth day of creation that he would make man. Not only would he make man, but man would be in God's own image and likeness, and man (*adam*) would be both male and female. In Genesis 2:21–24 we see the creation of Eve from Adam's rib and the institution of marriage at the beginning. All of this occurred before the fall. It is after the fall that we get the earliest and clearest statement in the Old Testament of the biological unity of all of humankind: "The man called his wife's name Eve, because she was the mother of all living" (Gen. 3:20). In one sense, the rest of the primeval history in Genesis 4–11 is a summary of the outworking of Genesis 3:20. It's a summary of how Eve really does become the mother of all living.

The physical descent of Adam is recorded for us in Genesis 5:1–3. The Scripture affirms two things in this post-fall account: (1) the *imago Dei* creation of man, and (2) that Seth is a son in Adam's own likeness and image (5:3). Adam is in God's image and likeness, and Seth is in Adam's image and likeness. With a superficial reading, Genesis 5:3 might seem to suggest that Seth was somehow made in some other image and likeness, as though the image and likeness of God was lost after the fall. But indeed it was not: "Whoever sheds the blood of man, by man shall his blood be shed, for God made man in his own image" (Gen. 9:6). After the fall and the universal flood of Noah's day, God reasserts the fact that all men are made in his image. God grounds the prohibition of murder in the fact that man after the fall and flood remain in his image and likeness. Then we come to Genesis 10, the Table of Nations. Historically and theologically the confusion regarding the notion of race begins here.

The Christian adoption of biological racial categories was at least in part a response to a perceived crisis in biblical authority. In the seventeenth, eighteenth, and nineteenth centuries, there grew a need to explain Genesis 10 in a way that protected biblical authority. Efforts were made to explain the existence of people outside the biblical world and in the New World. How did Native Americans end up in the Americas? How do we explain the antiquity of Chinese civilization? In what way are differing world religions corruptions of the religion of Noah? And why did Moses appear to know nothing about them?

In the mid to late eighteenth century, in an attempt to justify slavery, many ethnologists and theologians turned to Genesis 10 under the guise of the curse of Ham to find resources for articulating a theology and explanation of race and the apparent differences we all notice when we look around the room and for the theory of racial supremacy. Based on Genesis 10, heretical ideas like the Hamitic curse were offered. Over time the gradual reading of layers and layers of racialized assumptions onto the text of Scripture—particularly Genesis 10—reinforced the developing popular and scientific theories of racial origins.[2]

The Table of Nations came to be interpreted as a story of discontinuity. Attempts were made to answer the question, "Where do races come from?" But that is not the question the text answers. The text—if we take our cues from Scripture itself and not from issues outside Scripture—actually answers how Eve became the mother of all living. It's a story that includes the designation of people into clans, nations, and languages (10:5, 20, 31–32)—but not at the expense of their common genealogical ancestry. Notice that verse 32 serves as a bookend with verse 1 in the reference to Noah. From this one man via his three sons all "nations spread abroad on the earth after the flood."

Genesis 10 emphasizes the common origin and descent of all mankind and their geographic distribution across the Middle East,

North Africa, and the rest of the earth. I tend to think that this is the passage the apostle Paul has in mind when we read in Acts 17:26, "He made from one man every nation of mankind to live on all the face of the earth, having determined allotted periods and the boundaries of their dwelling place."

Race versus Ethnicity

In Genesis 10 we witness the rise of ethnicity or ethnic groups, not "race as biology." This is a critical distinction. "Race" is the theory, taking several forms, that there is an essential difference between people rooted in biological factors and manifested in things such as skin color, hair texture, eye shape and color, and a few other obvious markers. "Ethnicity," on the other hand, is a fluid construct that includes language, nationality or citizenship, cultural patterns, and perhaps religion. One way that race and ethnicity differ is that ethnicity is not rooted in biology as race theory historically has been.

"Race as biology" entrenches identity in physical appearance. Ethnicity is something that people of various physical appearances can permeate. So, for example, when we say someone is an "American Hindu" or a "Trinidadian Christian" we're talking about people of various skin colors and other physical characteristics sharing a set of religious, cultural, and social markers. We're talking about an ethnic identity definable apart from biology.

So let me stake a claim right now: one-half of the T4G speaking panel is black. We claim Ligon Duncan. Ligon has more knowledge of Earth, Wind and Fire and Bootsy Collins than most "bruthas" I know. At T4G 2006, Ligon received from me a lifetime ghetto pass. He can roll with me anywhere. I didn't give that pass to Mark. We claim C. J. Mahaney; C. J. is just plain cool. He's a brutha. And we claim John Piper. Piper preaches like a black man. He's a brutha. We don't claim Vanilla Ice. Ethnicity is not that permeable. This is a humorous way of illustrating something of the fluidity of ethnicity.

Biology does not determine ethnicity. Ethnicity may covary somewhat along phenotypical lines, but it does not depend on biological
assumptions the way race theory normally has.

The emphasis in the Old and New Testament wherever the Bible
speaks of creation of humankind is mankind's common biological
descent from Adam. Our common ancestry is underscored. The
most fundamental recognition is not our difference labeled "race"
but our oneness; not our *dis*continuity but *continuity* with one
another and with Adam and Eve, our first parents.

Let's put our thesis another way. The obvious truth that all
men are descended from Adam and Eve through the line of Noah
demands complete abandonment of "race as biological distinctiveness." Race—in the way we commonly use the term, as a proxy
for explaining differences in appearances—does not exist in truth.
I want to be clear. I am not saying that differences do not exist in
skin color, hair texture, and so on. I am saying that *the theory we
use to explain those differences*—the theory of biological races—is
completely false. Even much of the genetic and social scientific communities have abandoned the idea as a meaningful construct.[3] Our
identity problems begin with the wholesale adoption of this false
and unbiblical theory of racial distinctiveness.

My barber in the Caribbean looks just like me. You'd think
he was an African-American until he opens his mouth. When he
speaks, he speaks Jamaican patois so it is clear that he's not an
African-American. My administrative assistant is also proudly
Jamaican—very white-skinned. The lady in my barbershop looks a
lot like my wife. You might think she is African-American or even
Caymanian. She is Honduran. This notion of artificially imposing
categories on people according to color—biology—is sheer folly. It's
an impossibility. This is why much of the field on race and ethnicity
has largely abandoned the attempt to identify men based on biological categories of race.[4]

There is also a theological reason for abandoning the idea of race. The basis for human identity is our unity in Adam as his bio-logical descendants and as God's image bearers.

So What's the Big Deal?

G. K. Chesterton once said, "It isn't that we can't see the solution; it's that we can't see the problem." So much of our wrangling and struggling on racial issues stems from having misdiagnosed the problem. It comes from having accepted the faulty category of race and then forcibly trying to make it work in our relationships. What we need to do is dislodge this false idea from our thinking and affections.

There are six problems with race and a worldview built upon race that I want to mention. These six problems are not immediately apparent, but they warrant abandoning the idea of race.

1) *Race leads to the abuse of people and Scripture.* If we keep this category in our thinking, we leave insufficiently examined and incompletely refuted the gross tragedies and abuses of people and Scripture done in the name of race. It's critical that we recognize that we are not thinking about these issues from some objective, neutral starting point. We are actually in the hole, playing catch-up on this issue. Real and tremendous abuse and damage have already been done in the name of race. Allowing the unbiblical category of race to continue in our thinking only preserves and over-amplifies the sense of otherness and xenophobia that gives rise to racial preju-dice and racism.

Some people think that the way out of that history is to immerse ourselves in it or discuss it more and more as we see the day of Jesus' return approaching. Others suggest we not talk about it anymore at all, but they still want to continue viewing the world through a racial lens. Both poles are wrong; in fact, the entire spectrum is wrong. The most essential part of correcting the wrongs must be the destruction of the foundation that gave rise to it. It must mean the demolition of race as a construct.

2) *Once we accept race as a premise, it's a short walk to racism.* The moment we allow race into our thinking and combine that with our fallen heart, we have everything we need for each of us to be a most virulent racist. The difference between me and Louis Farrakhan, between my white friends and David Duke, is a matter of *degree* not *kind.* If I admit race in my thinking, what keeps me from espousing the kind of nonsense that Farrakhan espouses isn't some kind of superior morality. It's God's restraining grace. We simply haven't gone as far in our delusion and idolatry of self as Farrakhan or Duke has. Take it from a former committed racist: the trajectory of race is always toward racism and an unbridgeable otherness.

In terms of my personal experience, before Christ invaded my life I was committed to an Afrocentric view of the world. I looked to some notion of race and racial pride to define my identity and participation in the world. Fifteen years ago, as a college student, I was a committed Black Nationalist. Who I was back then makes Jeremiah Wright look like a poster child for the Boy Scouts. There was a time that my appearing at a gathering such as T4G was simply unthinkable, as was admitting to any kind of affection for whites. I had no need for white people whatsoever. I hated them bitterly. One of my favorite sayings was "some of my best friends have friends that are white." I would have told you that I wasn't a racist, that I could love African people or black people without hating white people. You would have seen me expressing love for blacks, not hatred for whites. I've heard skinheads, members of the Nation of Islam, evangelicals, and more garden variety people say things like this.

One of the high points of my more recent past was the privilege of speaking at the Twin Lakes Fellowship in Jackson, Mississippi. Twin Lakes is an annual gathering of PCA pastors, which is a polite way of saying there weren't many bruthas there. In the middle of the talk, it occurred to me where I was—an African-American with two hundred white men—in Mississippi in the woods at night. Now, you know that Jesus did that! Getting me from my racist past down to the woods of Mississippi was a supernatural demonstration of the power of the risen Christ.

3) *Race hinders or prevents meaningful engagement with others*. If we retain the idea of race in our thinking, we will never be able to get down to the more fluid and useful view of ethnicity and, thereby, will never be freed to carefully, critically, and prayerfully engage people, ideas, and culture. Race enslaves, and if we don't abandon it, we will be shackled in its prisons for a long time to come.

Have you ever felt a carnivorous gnawing in the pit of your stomach whenever a conversation turns to race? Have you ever felt, "Oh no! I don't want to go *there*. I don't want to talk about *this*"? That feeling or fear does not come simply from your concern about "messing up" by saying the wrong things. That feeling is not fundamentally about our incompetence at dealing with race, as though the only issue is our lack of education and skill. It's deeper than that. That feeling is the bitter bile of race itself leaking in our stomachs. The feeling comes from within the construct of race itself.

The idea of race proves to be inherently ad hominem. It is inherently "against the man." If we hold that we are different and are determined to be different by our biology, and if we cement that perceived difference with closely associated things such as culture, values, and ideas, then we can see why any time we critically try to engage those cultures, ideas, and values, the situation becomes volatile and explosive. It becomes volatile because most people experience a critique of culture and values as a comment *against them*, against their person. If we root culture, worldview, and ideas in biology, race instantaneously becomes ad hominem. It's instantly dangerous to talk about. It has within a kind of self-destruct mechanism so that when we push it with our tongues by speaking about it, we hear a "tick . . . tick . . . tick" as we wait for the major explosion.

But if ethnicity is permeable, if it is freed from the locus of body, it can be raised to the light, turned, and examined. We can discuss it prayerfully and critically. We can raise up hip-hop culture, Scottish culture, and grunge in Seattle, for example, and discuss them meaningfully, while lowering the risk of appearing to attack people by divorcing them from race. Abandoning race matters for our ability to talk to each other.

This is one reason the distinction between race as biologically determined and ethnicity as a fluid construct matters not only theologically but practically. If "race as biology" is something that we assume to be real and that cannot change, then any comment on things deeply or meaningfully associated with race explodes in personal offense and animus. But if ethnicity is permeable and adaptable, then we can engage people and cultures and ideas for the gospel and the cause of Christ without fear and with the genuine boldness that comes from love.

4) *Race undermines the authority and sufficiency of Scripture.* If we agree that the Bible teaches there is one human race (the race of Adam) and we continue to hold onto the unbiblical doctrine of race as biology, what are we doing but denying the authority and sufficiency of Scripture in defining us? What else can we conclude?[5] Holding onto race is rebellion and unbelief.

5) *Accepting race is resisting the Holy Spirit.* The Holy Spirit moved holy men of old to record the Word of God. The Holy Spirit enlightens the minds of men to receive and understand the Word. The Holy Spirit conforms us to that Word and the image of Christ, who sanctifies us by the truth. If we cast off the Word by accepting the unbiblical notion of race instead of receiving with humility (James 1:21) the Bible's teaching about our oneness, we resist the normal, sanctifying, conforming work of the Spirit, who has prayerfully made the Word alive to us.

6) *Race undermines the gospel.* If we deny our common ancestry and relatedness in Adam, we may be pulling apart the fabric of

the gospel itself. We've seen that in the heretical theory of polygenesis, the idea that races have their origins in multiple sources, not just in Adam. We've seen it in the ghastly racist propaganda that says African peoples are descended from apes or are more nearly ape-like than any other people. How is this related to the gospel? If all people are not descended from Adam, then (a) not all people inherited Adam's sin, and (b) the atonement of Christ is limited in an unbiblical and unhelpful way, since he atones only for the race of Adam. Fall and redemption are theologically pushed to a corner of humanity rather than attributed to the whole. Race undermines the gospel.

And race undermines the work of missions. How many pastors are trying to encourage their people to pray, give, and go? And how many Christians do we suspect think that missions and missionaries belong only to the adventurous Indiana Jones types because, for them, "those people over there" are really quite "other" racially? If we allow the Scripture to remove the racial thinking that creates the perception of an unbridgeable gap, then the "Scripture has the benign capacity to render racial Otherness as a type of cousinage or remote kinship."[6] It reduces the perceived gap people think they must cross to communicate with others. It allows a kind of concourse that race breaks down.

Race-ing the World at the Speed of Thought

You see the mess this erroneous category of "race" causes. The way out of this quicksand is (a) admit and emphasize our common ancestry in Adam, and (b) deny anything that looks or sounds like "race as biology" the place of reality or organizing system in our worldview. Thinking in racial categories has been an automatic reflexive assumption for all of us. It seems as natural as breathing. But we must deny it that place in our lives.

Some readers will no doubt feel the implication of what I'm saying. You recognize that abandoning the idea of race blows everything up. If we abandon race and emphasize our unity in Adam, even at a pre-Christian level, it changes all of our behavior. For example, abandoning race:

- Removes the factor that leads to easy identification of friends and social groups;
- No longer works as a basis for choosing where we live;
- No longer serves as a limiting factor for marriage decisions;
- Changes hiring policies and preferences; and
- Establishes a new basis for hate crimes.

We don't know how to live without race, so it scares us to think about it, like a child who will not sleep without a security blanket.

Picture yourself walking into a lunchroom. You enter alone. There are two tables in the lunchroom. The table on your left includes a group of people unlike you, some ethnic other. The table on your right includes a group of people ethnically like you. What would you instinctively do? We gravitate toward those we perceive to be like us. What is the mental calculus behind that gravitation? What are the mental mathematics taking place that lead to that impulse? We enter the room; we look at the two tables with the two groups, and at the speed of thought we calculate "not like me" or "like me." Then we think, *Like me; therefore safe. Like me and safe; therefore, some benefits to be gained. Like me and safe; some benefits to be gained; and therefore the likelihood of some joy and peace from our commonality.* There is an opposite calculus going on simultaneously: *Not like me; not safe; no benefit to be gained; no joy to share.* This happens at the speed of thought for most of us.

When we walk into the lunchroom with differing groups, we want to replace that calculus with this: *Descended from Adam—like me. Made in the image of God—like me. Fallen sinners—like me.* It's the emphasis on *like me*—the heritage we share in Adam—that begins to lay for our feet a bridge to cross over "otherness."

It turns out that judging a man by the content of his character is an inefficient process. It takes time. It takes risk. Judging a man by the content of his character requires more of us than we commonly think. It requires us to jettison something that has been foundational to our worldview: the idea of biological otherness—race. We will never reach character if we don't push past race.

Second Base: Union with Christ

All that we've said about our common ancestry in Adam is a resource available to both Christian and non-Christian alike. Our shared ancestry in Adam is a basis and resource for shared identity and understanding apart from our religious background. But for the Christian, there is an even greater basis for unity across ethnic lines and the abandonment of race as a part of our worldview and spiritual life. That basis is our union in Jesus Christ.

When the Christian walks into that lunchroom, she or he sees two groups and thinks, *Descended from Adam—like me. Made in the image of God—like me. Fallen sinners—like me.* If we find that any of those persons in the lunchroom are Christians, we are able to say, *United to Christ—like me. Sharing his Spirit—like me. Received the promises of eternal life and everlasting joy—like me.* The Scriptures tell us that in Christ we are given everything that pertains to life and godliness (2 Pet. 1:3). I don't think escaping the problems of race is an exception.

The apostle Paul writes, "I have been crucified with Christ. It is no longer I who live, but Christ who lives in me. And the life I now live in the flesh I live by faith in the Son of God, who loved me and gave himself for me" (Gal. 2:20). The apostle taught this same union with Christ in Romans 8:11: "If the Spirit of him who raised Jesus from the dead dwells in you, he who raised Christ Jesus from the dead will also give life to your mortal bodies through his Spirit who dwells in you." But Paul's insight into this union with Christ comes first from the Lord's own teaching. For example, in John

17:20–26 the Lord petitions the Father for our union with him and the Father:

> I do not ask for these only, but also for those who will believe in me through their word, *that they may all be one, just as you, Father, are in me, and I in you, that they also may be in us*, so that the world may believe that you have sent me. The glory that you have given me I have given to them, *that they may be one even as we are one, I in them and you in me*, that they may become perfectly one, so that the world may know that you sent me and loved them even as you loved me. Father, I desire that they also, whom you have given me, may be with me where I am, to see my glory that you have given me because you loved me before the foundation of the world. O righteous Father, even though the world does not know you, I know you, and these know that you have sent me. I made known to them your name, and I will continue to make it known, *that the love with which you have loved me may be in them, and I in them.*

We are made one in God just as the Father is in the Son and the Son is in the Father (v. 21). The Father in the Son, the Son in the saints (v. 23). We have entered into the eternal fellowship of love shared between the Father and the Son from all eternity.

When we recognize and live out of our union with Christ, then we round second base and are in scoring position, and we have the opportunity to settle this identity conundrum, which, I think, is at the heart of so many of our problems.

The Difference Our Union Makes

What reality have we entered, when by the sovereign election of God, the regeneration of the Holy Spirit, and the gracious gifts of repentance and faith, we have our eyes opened to see and behold Jesus and to give ourselves to him as Prophet, Priest, and King, our Savior and Deliverer whom we trust and follow? What reality does that create? We find ourselves transformed into newness of life. It's surprising how often the New Testament reaches for the little adjective *new* to describe the reality we've come into in Christ.

Second Corinthians 5:14–18 describes this newness in Christ:

> For the love of Christ controls us, because we have concluded this: that one has died for all, therefore all have died; and he died for all, that those who live might no longer live for themselves but for him who for their sake died and was raised. From now on, therefore, we regard no one according to the flesh. Even though we once regarded Christ according to the flesh, we regard him thus no longer. Therefore, if anyone is in Christ, he is a new creation. The old has passed away; behold, the new has come. All this is from God, who through Christ reconciled us to himself and gave us the ministry of reconciliation.

Our viewpoint and life change from worldly to heavenly (v. 16). We no longer regard people according to the flesh. And everyone that is Christ's is a new creation (v. 17). This is God's doing—his plan and work. Our reality now is not simply that we share a lineage with Adam. It is much greater than that. If we are Christ's, as Sinclair Ferguson put it, "We are brothers and sisters together—for Christ's blood creates a deeper lineage than our genes."[7]

What is happening to us via that union with Christ? We—like Adam—were made in God's image and likeness. We—like and in Adam—distorted and corrupted that image in the fall. But now, in Christ, we are together being restored to the image and likeness of God. Christ Jesus is "the image of the invisible God" (Col. 1:15). "He is the radiance of the glory of God and the exact imprint of his nature" (Heb. 1:3). And now, "Those whom he foreknew he also predestined to be conformed to the image of his Son" (Rom. 8:29). "And we all, with unveiled face, beholding the glory of the Lord, are being transformed into the same image from one degree of glory to another. For this comes from the Lord who is the Spirit" (2 Cor. 3:18). Ephesians 4:24 tells us what it is to be renewed in the likeness of God when it exhorts us "to put on the new self, created after the likeness of God in true righteousness and holiness." Colossians 3:10 tells us we "have put on the new self, which is being renewed in knowledge after the image of its creator."

Christ has become our wisdom—our righteousness, holiness, and redemption—and he works in us to conform us to himself. On the basis of our union with and renewal in Christ, notice the application the word makes in Colossians 3:11: "Here there is not Greek and Jew, circumcised and uncircumcised, barbarian, Scythian, slave, free; but Christ is all, and in all." Even the natural ethnic distinctions, which are real and to be valued, are vastly secondary to this union that God has so wonderfully wrought in Christ. Our doctrine of man, which is to say, our understanding of ourselves and our true identity, must be determined and informed by our union with Christ in his person and work.

Union, Ethnicity, and Privilege

Our main project is not fundamentally to build shrines to ethnic achievement. To be clear, relaxing into ethnic privilege because we are the majority in our church or culture *is* a form of ethnic shrine building. It's ethnic shrine building because we presume upon privilege in a way that exalts our own ethnic culture above others. Our project in Christ is not shrine building for man-made culture, but to be living monuments of God's glory in Christ, bearing the renewed image and likeness of God more clearly through faith in Christ, and living in the divinely given culture found in the church—a culture of holiness and righteousness, justice and truth.

Failure to do this, I think, is the serious limitation of so many well-intentioned racial reconciliation efforts. Those efforts seem to me to major on race and to minor on Christ and his work, in too many cases. Some approaches seem to suggest that merely embracing the "other's" ethnicity and culture somehow enhances our embrace of Christ. I think the opposite is the way forward. It's as we tightly cling to Jesus that we find ourselves embracing other people clinging to the Savior. The cross reconciles men to God and men to each other.

Much of our difficulty in experiencing this oneness and new-ness in Christ comes from assuming that race is a theological and biological reality when it's not, and from assuming that race is something that cannot be shed and should not be shed but honored. We keep grasping for this mirage instead of tightening our grip on Jesus. That effort to grasp the mirage is hurting us.

Nothing I'm saying destroys ethnic identity but profoundly orients our identity in and toward the spiritual realities and accom-plishments of Christ on the cross. If ethnicity is a fluid construct, then what happens to the Christian is that he is poured out of the old jars of race and distilled and poured into the new jar of Christ. Our natural ethnic identities, already permeable, give way to our new identity. We become Christ-ians, a new spiritual ethnic group. We gather by that family and clan and nation and speak the lan-guage of Zion. That's what we're after.

Third Base: Unity in the Church

We move to third base by asking, "Where is this new spiritual reality in Christ to be housed or displayed?" Where can it be observed? Where is this dynamic available for us to witness, see, and touch?

It is not available in coffee houses. The local Rotary club does not display it. Neither do neighborhood or community groups, political parties, governmental jurisdictions, nor even pastor fra-ternals and networks, as valuable as they are. The church penulti-mately displays the unity we have in Christ, the oneness we share with him and with each other. The local church is the display before the ultimate display. The local church is not a perfect display; we want to be careful to avoid an over-realized eschatology. But an over-realized eschatology doesn't really seem to be our problem when it comes to identity.

It seems to me that our problem leans in the other direction. We need to live more fully in the already. We live beneath our inheritance in Christ. If Esau sold his inheritance for a bowl of porridge, we've sold an even greater inheritance for his leftovers. If the prodigal squandered his inheritance, we're the older brother refusing to rejoice and receive our once-dead sibling.

Ultimately, the one new-man reality that transcends gender, ethnicity, and class accomplished by Christ in the cross awaits its full display in the new heavens and the new earth when we gather around the throne and fall before the Lamb. But we are to get glimpses of that glorious future in our local congregations. Consider Ephesians 2:14–16 (NIV):

> For he himself is our peace, who has made the two one and has destroyed the barrier, the dividing wall of hostility, by abolishing in his flesh the law with its commandments and regulations. His purpose was to create in himself one new man out of the two, thus making peace, and in this one body to reconcile both of them to God through the cross, by which he put to death their hostility.

Note the past-tense nature of many of these verbs: "*has made* the two one"; "*has destroyed* the barrier." This work of making Jew and Gentile one new man was accomplished on the cross in a very real way when the sinless Savior died as atonement for sin. There are present tense verbs as well: "He *is* our peace." Peace is a Person. It's Jesus Christ. This peace is experienced in him, in his body, in the church. It is an existing peace accomplished on the cross.

We can see more of these present-tense realities accomplished by Christ and housed in the church. "The Gentiles *are* heirs together with Israel, members together of one body, and sharers together in the promise in Christ Jesus" (Eph. 3:6 NIV). It is understandable then that Paul goes on to exhort the church at Ephesus to a practical, real unity in Ephesians 4:1–6. For the following reasons, I doubt that Paul now means in chapter 4 that church unity is acceptably limited and rationed by skin color:

- Paul describes the work of Christ in its abolition of the "dividing wall of hostility" between Jew and Gentile.
- Paul describes this reconciliation of Jew and Gentile in the body of Christ, in his flesh through the cross.
- Paul describes all of this reality as a demonstration of God's manifold wisdom to the rulers and authorities of the heavenly realm.

I don't think Jesus is impressed with our failure in our churches to love others who are unlike us. That's just not going to be compelling in glory in light of the fact that the loving Savior died for enemies, rebels, and wretches who were anything *but* like him. Our local churches are to be the penultimate display of the new humanity created in Christ Jesus.

The Homogeneous Unit Principle and Loveless Churches

Many readers of this volume will reject the "homogeneous unit principle" as a betrayal of the Bible's depiction of the church. Yet, how many of us practically affirm that principle every Sunday morning when we drive past churches filled with people "not like us" to get to the one where everybody looks "like us"? Even if we are not committed to the homogeneous unit principle theologically, it does seem that far too many of us are committed in our practice. Our church membership *may* only be the practical affirmation of our unspoken but resolutely practiced commitment to racializing the church where Christ does not.

This is not merely a problem of integration, of spiritual forced busing to churches. It's more serious than that. From Sunday to

Sunday, month to month, year after year, Christians of every hue are abandoning one another in lovelessness. Because of our loveless behavior, race seems so overpowering of an idea—even though it is not real. Our love seems to seek convenience and familiarity and to be bounded by the ease that race offers, when Christ calls us to a largeness and breadth of love that is like his own, which assembles and gathers and loves and gives to every nation, tribe, and language, to be displayed in our churches. Christ has made us one and called us to unity, but we have filed a declaration of independence from one another and voluntarily enacted Jim Crow practices to reinforce it.

Is there any biblical justification for the socially and ethnically stratified existence of the American church? Even if the fulfillment awaits the final things, shouldn't we incline ourselves to living and experiencing more and more of that reality while we wait? Article XVII of the T4G Affirmations and Denials reads:

> We affirm that God calls his people to display his glory in the recon-
> ciliation of the nations within the Church, and that God's pleasure
> in this reconciliation is evident in the gathering of believers from
> every tongue and tribe and people and nation. We acknowledge that
> the staggering magnitude of injustice against African-Americans in
> the name of the Gospel presents a special opportunity for display-
> ing the repentance, forgiveness, and restoration promised in the
> Gospel. We further affirm that evangelical Christianity in America
> bears a unique responsibility to demonstrate this reconciliation
> with our African-American brothers and sisters.
>
> We deny that any church can accept racial prejudice, discrimi-
> nation, or division without betraying the Gospel.

We believe that. How now shall we live that?

Seminarian, will you join or apply to serve as a pastor in a church full of people you previously thought were "not like you"? Church planter, will you consider a merger or takeover of a fledgling congregation full of people you previously thought were "not like you"? Church member, will you move to a church faithful to the gospel and closer to your home, even though you're going to be a minority in that congregation?

Pastor, how now shall you preach? Even if you are from a place that really is mono-ethnic, will you preach to your people in such a way as to encourage them to recognize their union with all others in Adam and with all Christians in Christ? Will you preach in such a way that young Sally or Johnny will not be overwhelmed when immersed in a college environment with all kinds of people because you have explained that those other people are really her or his brothers and sisters in Adam, if not in Christ? Will you preach in such a way as to bring to life in full color, in all of its shape and glory, God's purpose to assemble to himself people from every tribe and nation? Will you make that biblical impulse clear to your people, even if you're not in diverse settings? Will you include in the course of your preaching those thoughts and applications that help your people abandon the bankrupt, love-curtailing notion of race to live unified in the body of Christ?

Home Plate: Unity in Glory

All that the Scripture teaches us and calls us to be is intended to fit us for the final stretch and for reaching home base. As pastors, it's our job to fit our people for heaven. We are to use all that the Spirit gives us to pack and push and shove our people up into Christ. We're to whet their spiritual appetites for the delicacies of glory and to stir their hearts for the fellowship of the Beloved. We are to prepare our people to sing the new song of Revelation 5:9–10: "Worthy are you to take the scroll and to open its seals, for you were slain, and by your blood you ransomed people for God from every tribe and language and people and nation, and you have made them a kingdom and priests to our God, and they shall reign on the earth."

All of human history is headed to this one reality—a new kingdom of priests, one in Christ, redeemed by his blood, serving the one true and living God. If that's where we're headed, why not live more like that now?

CHAPTER 3

THE SINNER NEITHER WILLING NOR ABLE

John MacArthur

Before I dig into my subject, I want to say what a privilege it is to minister to people with a passion for getting the gospel right. You are the most important people in the world because the world's greatest hope is the gospel. The most important people don't run nations, institutions, corporations, or universities, because entities such as those cannot make an eternal difference by themselves. Those who preach the gospel as Jesus did are more important than kings, presidents, and prime ministers.

It is therefore critical that we understand the nature of our message and the foundations of our gospel. That's what prompted me to address the subject of total depravity—fallen humanity's unwillingness and inability to love God, obey him, or please him in any way. This is a major gospel theme.

In John 5:39–40 our Lord says, "You search the Scriptures because you think that in them you have eternal life; it is these that testify about Me; and you are unwilling to come to Me so that you may have life."[1] He was saying that those who search the Scriptures with a view toward eternal life—Scriptures that bear unstinting testimony to Christ as Savior and Lord—are nonetheless *unwilling* to come to him. Why? Because of their depravity.

Depravity the Most Despised Doctrine

Jesus also said, "No one *can* come to Me unless the Father who sent Me draws him" (John 6:44). He is presenting here the doctrine of human unwillingness and inability, which is perhaps the most thoroughly despised doctrine in all the Bible. The idea that sinners are completely helpless to redeem themselves (or even make any contribution to their redemption from sin and divine judgment) is a distinctly Christian doctrine, contrary to all non-Christian views of man or humankind.

All the major religions in the world apart from biblical Christianity are based on the notion that righteousness is gained by good works. At their core is the idea that people can be good enough either to merit the favor of some deity or at least to enjoy a happy afterlife. Therefore, in one way or another, all false systems of religion teach that redemption hinges on human ability, human works, human willpower, self-atonement, or the supposed basic goodness of humanity. Naturally, then, all of them are compelled in one sense or another to deny the totality of mankind's depravity.

One of the inevitable features of universal human fallenness is self-deception about one's true condition, based on the dominating reality of human pride. Practically every sinner is convinced (to some degree) that he is fundamentally good—or at the very least, that he isn't quite as bad as someone else. Of course, most people are apt to admit, casually, that they're not perfect. A few might even acknowledge that they actually sin against God. But hardly any will admit that they are truly evil. They have no ability to see any evil in their good, and they especially tend not to acknowledge any evil in their religion. They therefore cannot admit—even to themselves— that they are incurably evil, hostile to God, and utterly incapable of any true good.

People will go to almost any length to try to obscure or paper over their depravity. Many even invoke the name of the one true God and Father of our Lord Jesus Christ and claim to love him, while in reality they detest him. They may have a genuine but senti-mental affection for some god of their own making, suited to their own preferences—and often they will even call that imaginary god by the name of the true God—but they actually hate and cannot love the God of both the Old and New Testaments. Their refusal to acknowledge the true extent of their own wickedness is proof of their unbelief.

In fact, no sin could possibly be more heinous than such a refusal to love God as he truly is. It entails a breach of both the first and second commandments, starting with a failure to love the Lord our God with a whole heart and have no other gods before him, and then compounding the error by worshiping one's own imaginary image instead of bowing to the true God of Scripture. The tendency to invent false gods and insist they are the true God—the sin of idolatry—is another universal trait of fallen humanity, and it is one more vivid proof of how utterly depraved the human heart really is.

Even when people have flagrant sins that are exposed in undeni-able ways, or when they are otherwise compelled to confess some specific evil in their lives, they still will usually steadfastly deny that they are so thoroughly evil as to be unable to redeem themselves (or at least contribute something of merit to their redemption). Even the most grotesque sinners often blithely imagine that God will never actually judge them or hold them eternally accountable for their sins. They'll often insist they really aren't so bad after all.

Conversely, the godliest people are invariably those who are most aware of their own depravity. The most humble and spiritually minded saints are actually more conscious of the sin in their hearts and lives—and more ready to confess it—than some of the most wicked evildoers the world has ever seen. John Bunyan, for exam-ple, author of the classic *The Pilgrim's Progress*, said in his spiritual autobiography, *Grace Abounding to the Chief of Sinners*, "The best prayer I ever prayed had enough sin in it to damn the whole world." The prophet Isaiah, using unusually strong language in Hebrew, wrote, "All our righteous deeds are like a filthy garment" (Isa. 64:6). Isaiah was describing a kind of defilement so vile it's not normally mentioned in polite society—an uncleanness so thoroughly defiling and so permanently staining that garments contaminated in such a way needed to be destroyed rather than laundered. And notice: that's the biblical appraisal of the *good* things we do—our righteous deeds, not our most sinful ones.

I am deeply concerned, because many evangelical spokesmen today seem to hate the truth of total depravity. They often bend over backward to avoid it. You'll sometimes hear preachers simply echoing worldly notions about self-esteem and positive thinking, as if those were biblical and spiritual ideas. Nothing could be further from the truth. The view that people are fundamentally good actually betrays a hatred of the God of Scripture—because such a message deceives sinners about their sinfulness, and it hides the true God behind a benign, domesticated god of some worldly psychologist's making.

In fact, depravity is often most minimized in the very contexts where it should be proclaimed with the utmost clarity. Remember, the notion that man has enough goodness in him to contribute in some way to his salvation is one of the foundational errors of all false religion. Of all the errors that need to be most clearly refuted today, at the head of the list is the popular notion that the sinner's real problem is low self-esteem—so his perspective of himself simply needs to be pumped up. In major segments of evangelicalism, that idea has been adopted, baptized, and blessed with spiritual-sounding benedictions. It has even become the basis of manipulative church-growth strategies.

This is no minor problem. Those who reject, despise, minimize, or ignore the doctrine of depravity have done as much to impede the advance of the gospel as open enemies of the cross. (That is not to say they're all not Christians, but it is to say they're profoundly confused at best.) To grasp the truth of human depravity is to begin to understand all the other doctrinal components of salvation. Once you grasp the significance of human depravity, all the other major principles of grace and redemption soon become obvious. Most of all, if you see the reality of depravity, you must then see that true gospel ministry transcends all forms of manipulation and is *purely* a divine work. The doctrine of human depravity therefore honors God completely like no other truth, because it leaves absolutely no honor for man in regard to salvation.

The Historical Perspective on the Doctrine of Depravity

If you entered the evangelical world of today for the first time, you probably would get the impression that the doctrine of depravity is a recent arrival—because the notion of human free will is so wildly popular. Indeed, when people today hear the doctrine of total depravity, they often think it's something new and rather radical. They assume that the idea of man's free will and his ability to lay hold of salvation by simply making an independent choice to do so is biblically orthodox, because the gospel is so commonly presented in those terms. But the fact is, the Bible's clear teaching on original sin and human depravity has been essential to Christian orthodoxy from the beginning. It was not invented in modern times, nor was it invented by John Calvin or Martin Luther. The doctrine was affirmed by all the important church fathers, and it was not even controversial until Pelagius attacked it in the early fifth century. The truth of depravity was often eclipsed by medieval scholastics because of their extreme sacramental emphasis, but all the major Reformers defended the doctrine and brought it back to the forefront of the church's thinking.

Pelagius insisted that any sinner who chooses to obey God can do so by sheer willpower. He denounced a passage in Augustine's *Confessions* in which Augustine prayed to God for grace in order to enable him to obey. Pelagius protested that such a prayer constituted a denial of human responsibility. That launched an extensive controversy, and as the debate progressed, Pelagius and his most vocal disciple, Celestius, worked themselves into the untenable position of claiming that human nature is in no way defiled or disabled by inherited sin. They insisted that every person has perfect freedom of will, just as Adam did. So if we sin, they said, it is purely by choice, not because of any corruption or inability in our fallen nature. In effect, they denied the doctrine of original sin as well as the truth of total depravity. Pelagianism was formally denounced at the Council of Ephesus in AD 431.

But the Pelagianizing principle was by no means dead. A new wave followed with the compromise idea that Adam's sin had in *some* measure affected and disabled all men, but sinners were still left with just enough freedom of will to make the first move of faith toward God. At that point, they claimed, God's grace is given in response to the sinner's choice. Notice how that puts the sinner, not God, in the driver's seat, and makes human choice the determinative factor in salvation. That view is known as semi-Pelagianism. The idea is that depravity is real, but it is not *total* (affecting every aspect of a person—mind, emotions, and will). Saving grace from God then becomes a divine response rather than the efficient cause of our salvation. Semi-Pelagianism was also soundly denounced by several church councils, starting with the council of Orange in 529.

Luther's great treatise *The Bondage of the Will*, in which he wrestled with the humanist scholar Erasmus to defend the doctrine of depravity, was built on what the apostle Paul, Augustine, John Wycliffe, John Huss, and William Tyndale had all affirmed before him. John Calvin defends this biblical truth as the first point in his *Institutes of the Christian Religion* (1536), describing it as the necessary foundation of sound anthropology and soteriology. The Westminster Confession (1647) says, "Man, by his fallen state of sin, has wholly lost all ability of will to any spiritual good accompanying salvation." You find similar affirmations in the Belgic

Confession (1561), the Anglican Thirty-nine Articles (1563), and the London Baptist Confession (1644). This is a historic doctrine.

The Biblical Truth Regarding Human Depravity

Having surveyed the past, let's consider afresh what Scripture says. When the Bible speaks about the condition of the sinner, what does it say?

The terminology is stark. The Bible often employs the language of death; sometimes darkness, blindness, hardness, slavery, incurable sickness, and alienation. The Holy Scriptures are clear that depravity is a condition that affects the entire body, mind, emotions, desires, motives, will, and behavior. It is a condition of total, helpless bondage. No sinner unaided by God can ever overcome it.

Despite that obvious truth, pragmatism dominates the professing church. *Theology* has been replaced by or subverted by *methodology*. Throughout history, denominations have been established and defined in terms of doctrine, but today the stress is on style and technique. Much of current evangelical strategy merely aims only to identify what people most desire, and then tells them Jesus will give it to them if they would but choose him. God is portrayed as sitting in heaven, wringing his hands and loving everyone intensely yet frustrated when people won't come to him for the things they desire. Few seem to consider that what the unconverted sinner actually desires is the last thing God wants to give him—and what the gospel actually says about fallen humanity is the last thing sinners want to hear. Some very familiar texts deal with this. Let's start with Ephesians 2:

> You were dead in your trespasses and sins, in which you formerly walked according to the course of this world, according to the prince of the power of the air, of the spirit that is now working in the sons of disobedience. Among them we too all formerly lived in the lusts of our flesh, indulging the desires of the flesh and of

the mind, and were by nature children of wrath, even as the rest. (vv. 1–3)

The prepositional phrase "by nature" in verse 3 can also be translated "by birth."

We have inherited a corrupt nature from Adam. Paul's epistle to the Romans is clear that "through one man sin entered into the world, and death through sin, and so death spread to all men, because all sinned" (5:12). First Corinthians 15 is rightly called the resurrection chapter, and here is a clue why: "Since by a man came death, by a man also came the resurrection of the dead. For as in Adam all die, so also in Christ all will be made alive" (vv. 21–22). We have all literally inherited death; and death epitomizes the corruption Adam's sin passed to his progeny. We are sinners by nature from birth. That explains why you don't have to teach children to disobey; that comes naturally to all of us.

The human condition is a profound state of depravity, driven by "the lust of the flesh and the lust of the eyes and the boastful pride of life" (1 John 2:16).

If anything is to change us, it must be the grace of God. That is why Ephesians 2:4–5 is such good news: "But God, being rich in mercy, because of His great love with which He loved us, even when we were dead in our transgressions, made us alive together with Christ (by grace you have been saved)." This is a divine miracle in which God makes the dead alive!

Ephesians 4:18 describes unbelievers as "being darkened in their understanding, excluded from the life of God because of the ignorance that is in them, because of the hardness of their heart." It is a condition from which the sinner cannot recover on his own. Colossians 2:13 declares, "When you were dead in your transgressions and the uncircumcision of your flesh, He made you alive." God commands and life comes. This is analogous to the resurrection of Lazarus, who was dead for four days before the Lord called him to walk out of his tomb. There was no residual spark of life in Lazarus that contributed to his resurrection. Without the living Christ, he was as helpless as any other corpse. We are a race of Lazaruses, dependent upon the grace of God for new life.

This is foundational truth. It's also a truth that *permeates* Scripture, including some familiar texts you may never have associated with the doctrine of depravity. John 1:12–13 declares, "As many as received Him, to them He gave the right to *become* children of God, even to those who believe in His name, who were born, not of . . . the will of man, but of God." No one is born a child of God, but must become one.

That is precisely what Jesus tried to explain to Nicodemus: "Truly, truly, I say to you, unless one is born again he cannot see the kingdom of God" (John 3:3). Nicodemus picks up on Jesus' word picture and asks, "How can a man be born again when he is old?" (v. 4). He understands that man has no capability to bring birth to himself, but the truth that he was fallen and in need of a new birth was as hard for Nicodemus as it is for you and me. (In fact, Nicodemus was a Pharisee, and the doctrine of depravity was especially odious to Pharisees, because they had more personally invested in trying to earn divine favor through good works than anyone.) So Jesus responded, "Truly, truly I say to you, unless one is born of water and the Spirit"—a reference to Ezekiel 36:25–27 about spiritual cleansing and regeneration—"he cannot enter into the kingdom of God. That which is born of the flesh is flesh, and that which is born of the Spirit is spirit," so the flesh cannot produce spiritual life. "Do not be amazed that I said to you, 'You must be born again'" (vv. 5–7). Nicodemus, however, was both amazed and confused, saying, "How can these things be?" (v. 9).

Notice what Jesus *doesn't* say. He doesn't say, "Here are four steps," or, "Pray this prayer after me." But what he *does* say in verse 8 is absolutely shocking to anyone whose confidence might be in human free will: "The wind blows where it wishes and you hear the sound of it, but do not know where it comes from and where it is going; so is everyone who is born of the Spirit." What kind of answer is that? Our Lord is saying, "Spiritual birth is not up to you; it's up to the Holy Spirit, and you have no control over where or when the Spirit moves."

Salvation is a divine work. It has to be, since flesh just produces flesh. Dead people can't give themselves life. The Spirit gives life to whom he will. You can see when it happens, but you can't make it happen. Jesus, in John 5:21, declares, "Just as the Father raises the dead and gives them life, even so the Son also gives life to whom He wishes." The Father, Son, and Holy Spirit are in agreement that this is a work of divine power. Perhaps nowhere does Jesus make that clearer than in John 6:44: "No one can come to Me unless the Father who sent Me draws him." The Good News from our Lord's own lips is that "if the Son makes you free [from sin], you will be free indeed" (John 8:36).

In none of those texts, by the way, did Jesus ever defend the sinner's ability. Yes, the sinner has a *kind* of free will, in the sense that we aren't compelled to choose by any external force or compulsion. But as Luther clarified in *Bondage of the Will*, the sinner will always choose according to his strongest desires. In other words, his choices don't determine the state of his heart; the state of his heart determines how he will choose. What is the fallen human heart like? Jesus said, "From within, out of the heart of men, proceed the evil thoughts, fornications, thefts, murders, adulteries, deeds of coveting and wickedness, as well as deceit, sensuality, envy, slander, pride and foolishness. All these evil things proceed from within and defile the man" (Mark 7:21–23). Here is an Old Testament summary of the same truth: "The heart is more deceitful than all else and is desperately sick" (Jer. 17:9). The King James Version gives an even more forceful rendition: "The heart is deceitful above all things, and *desperately wicked*." Is there anything we can do to heal ourselves? "Can the Ethiopian change his skin or the leopard his spots? Then you also can do good who are accustomed to doing evil" (Jer. 13:23). One's skin color or an animal's pelt design is morally neutral, but the human heart is not. None are changeable apart from divine intervention.

Along with the heart, the human mind is corrupt every way possible. It also is unwilling and unable "because the mind set on the flesh is hostile toward God; for it does not subject itself to the law of God, for it is not even able to do so, and those who are in the flesh cannot please God" (Rom. 8:7–8). Perhaps that's the most definitive text of all regarding the sinner's absolute inability and unwillingness to acknowledge the true God on his own. The sinner is unable also to acknowledge the gospel on his own: "A natural man does not accept the things of the Spirit of God, for they are foolishness to him; and he cannot understand them, because they are spiritually appraised" (1 Cor. 2:14). The truth is, "No one can say, 'Jesus is Lord,' except by the Holy Spirit" (1 Cor. 12:3). Sadly, "the god of this world has blinded the minds of the unbelieving so that they might not see the light of the gospel of the glory of Christ, who is the image of God" (2 Cor. 4:4).

What can remedy that? The apostle Paul answers that question in the next verse: "We do not preach ourselves but Christ Jesus as Lord, and ourselves as your bond-servants for Jesus' sake" (v. 5). What happens when we're faithful to do that? "God, who said, 'Light shall shine out of darkness'" on the first day of creation, will shine a light in our hearts "to give the Light of the knowledge of the glory of God in the face of Christ" (v. 6). Again, it's a divine miracle. The heart and the mind are affected and infected by depravity, but God is willing to bring healing through the gospel.

Human beings are naturally religious, but not in the good sense of the word. In Romans 1:23, the apostle Paul explains the same phenomenon we discussed earlier—how we tend to blaspheme by substituting the true God with a false one of our own invention (or we blindly go along with someone else's false god). None of us is excluded. The bottom line is this: "There is none righteous, not even one; there is none who understands . . . none who seeks for God" (Rom. 3:10–11, citing Ps. 14:1–3). Both the Old and New Testaments make it crystal clear that we have no potential, no capability, no hope on our own. The sum is that man is evil and selfish, unwilling and unable because he is dead. He loves his sin and attempts to soothe his conscience by meeting the low standards of his invented god. Because man is made in the image of God, he may occasionally recognize sin for what it is but only in its grosser forms. Meanwhile, he will miss a world of damning subtlety.

We have been referring to this doctrine as "total depravity." That expression can be somewhat confusing, because it might seem to suggest that every sinner is as thoroughly vicious or twisted as it is possible to be. Yet clearly, that is not the case. Not all sinners are rapists or serial killers. Some manage to seem pretty good by comparison. Some are philanthropists and some are great artists. We were made in the image of God, and that image is still indelibly stamped on us—damaged but not utterly eradicated. We all have talents and abilities and human affections that can look very good and make us seem admirable. Furthermore, the principle of common grace restrains the full expression of human depravity. So the world itself, for the most part, is in some state of order, not complete anarchy. Obviously, then, we're not as bad as we could be when it comes to the *manifestation* of our fallenness.

Many people therefore insist that there must be some residual good left untainted in the sinner that can help bring about his or her salvation. Surely there is some divine spark in us that can redeem us. If we would simply refuse to think of ourselves as bad, there's no limit to the good we might do. That's the theme of countless self-help books and metaphysical seminars. It's the religion of Oprah and Norman Vincent Peale. That same kind of thinking is also all too prevalent in the contemporary church.

But Scripture is clear about the extent of our depravity: "The whole head is sick and the whole heart is faint. From the sole of the foot even to the head there is nothing sound in it" (Isa. 1:5–6). The word *total* in the expression "total depravity" refers to the fact that sin has so thoroughly infected us that no part of our being—mind, affections, or will—is free from the taint of sin. We're totally *dead* spiritually. Like an array of corpses ranging from freshly dead to thoroughly decomposed, some may be in a more advanced state of putrefaction than others, but all are equally dead. Our inability is total, too, because there is absolutely nothing we can do to earn our salvation. If we are to be awakened from that death and redeemed from our sin, God must do it, and God alone.

John Calvin affirmed that truth, and the church of his era grew as a result. But not everyone liked what they heard. The Arminian Remonstrants formally recognized that Scripture says sinners are fallen and helpless apart from the grace of God. But they found it hard to reconcile that idea with the truth of human responsibility (which is likewise clearly taught in the Bible). Their solution to the dilemma was the hypothesis of "prevenient grace." The idea is that God gives all people just enough grace to restore their power to choose whether to accept or reject Christ—and how they choose determines whether they will be saved or not. Of course, the Bible says nothing about universal prevenient grace, but that is the Arminian way of restoring the power of choice to every sinner without formally denying the truth that sinners are spiritually dead.

To their credit, most Arminians want to give all the glory to God in salvation, but they also want to believe sinners can initiate the process of their own salvation. Those are mutually exclusive goals. Nevertheless, the illogical thinking arising from that contradiction has literally taken over and shaped the dominant system of thought in evangelical Christianity for over a century. It is the principle behind most revivalism, and it also is the idea that motivates the kind of evangelism that attempts to woo the sinner to decide for Christ rather than declaring the sinner's dire need to repent and seek God's mercy and grace through Christ. That accounts for the stubborn and widespread belief that sinners have it in their power to respond to God on their own free-will initiative—as if sinners were sovereign and God needed the assent of their wills in order to save them.

Those are ideas you will not find anywhere in Scripture. The Bible plainly and repeatedly teaches that the sinner is both unable and unwilling to make the first move, because he is a hardened rebel lacking any spiritual life or any godly desires. At best, he will make a false move toward God based upon his own fallen desires and motivated by some self-aggrandizing incentive. When Christians try to tell people God wants to give them whatever they want if only they will come to him, they are actually hiding the truth about God's glorious, sovereign nature and compounding the sinner's self-deception. Regeneration is not synergistic (a two-way cooperative effort) but monergistic (a one-way act of God). If it were not a work of God alone, we would be doomed, because the fall has rendered us totally unable to cooperate with him or contribute anything of saving value to the work God does for us.

In regeneration we neither resist nor cooperate. We are acted upon. We are changed by the Holy Spirit, not apart from our will but through our will by his illuminating our minds so we understand and believe the gospel. We believe not because we had more sense than the people who refuse the gospel but because God graciously made the first move and opened our hearts to heed his Word and believe it (cf. Acts 16:14). There's nothing for us to be subtly proud of but only profoundly grateful for.

I wonder how this text would go down at the next revival or evangelist training meeting: "The Lord's bond-servant must not be quarrelsome, but be kind to all, able to teach, patient when wronged, with gentleness correcting those who are in opposition, *if perhaps God may grant them repentance leading to the knowledge of the truth*, and they may come to their senses and escape from the snare of the devil, having been held captive by him to do his will" (2 Tim. 2:24–26).

That is the historic doctrine that has been affirmed through the centuries. Titus 3:3–7 explains that we all start life foolish, "disobedient, deceived, enslaved to various lusts and pleasures, spending our life in malice and envy, hateful, hating one another. But when the kindness of God our Savior and His love for mankind appeared, He saved us, not on the basis of deeds which we have done in righteousness, but according to His mercy, by the washing of regeneration and renewing by the Holy Spirit, whom He poured out upon us richly through Jesus Christ our Savior, so that being justified by His grace we would be made heirs according to the hope of eternal life." Amen! What can we do in response but praise him for his grace and live for his glory?

The Implications behind the Doctrine of Depravity

Flat denial of total depravity has been a staple of America's religious culture for well over a century. It is at the heart of both modernism and theological liberalism, which de-emphasized theology and exalted philanthropic deeds. Churches that went that way wanted the fruit but severed the root, so they withered and died. Witness the condition of mainline denominations that embraced modernist thinking. All of them are spiritual wastelands today.

The emergent movement is currently positioning itself to repeat the same mistake. Its foundation is neo-liberalism, so its leaders say things like, "We don't know what the Bible means—nobody does, so let's just be like Jesus in the world and help the poor and disenfranchised." They are not preaching the same gospel he preached, but they are shrewd enough not to jettison the "evangelical" label because they want access to the churches that old-line liberalism has not already utterly dissipated. The term *evangelical* is quickly becoming meaningless, so instead of depending on it or any other label, remember what Jesus said in the Sermon on the Mount: "Every good tree bears good fruit, but the bad tree bears bad fruit. . . . Every tree that does not bear good fruit is cut down and thrown into the fire. So then, you will know them by their fruits" (Matt. 7:17–20).

The gurus of the church-growth movement who canonized pragmatic methodologies for attracting unchurched people were the middle modernists, between the old and the new, bearing the same bad fruit: a plethora of church programs and preaching styles designed to ape the world and feed sensual appetites. All of these movements have de-emphasized theology, but there's still an incipient Arminianism underlying all of them—inherent in the belief that somehow sinners will respond better if our methods change. We have to be careful of that. Because people think salvation is a result of sinners' own free-will decisions for Christ, they tell sinners what they *want* to hear to try to get them to *like* him—and that in turn has obscured the gospel rather than unleashing it to do the true work of salvation.

We must recognize that the fallen sinner hates the true God and fatally loves himself. Of course he wants a god who will give him what he wants! The gospel, however, assaults the sinner's self-worship, self-assurance, self-esteem, and smugness, shattering his confidence in his religion and his spirituality. It crushes him under the full weight of God's law with a verdict of guilty. The only way he can be set free is if he comes to loathe himself and all his ambitions, repent of his sins, and love the one true God, whom Holy Scripture reveals to be the God and Father of our Lord Jesus Christ.

That is the message under which God awakens the sinner and leads him to repentance and faith. Never appeal to that which enslaves the sinner—materialism, sex, pleasure, personal ambition, a better life, success, or whatever—in an effort to convince the sinner of his need to be rescued from the very enslavement you're appealing to. Instead, call the sinner to flee from all that is natural, all that so powerfully enslaves him, and urge him to come to the cross to be saved from eternal judgment.

Soft preaching makes hard people. If you preach a soft gospel, you'll have hard, selfish people. If you preach hard truth, it will break hard hearts, like when the apostle Peter preached on the day of Pentecost to the very people who crucified Christ and "they were pierced to the heart, and said to Peter and the rest of the apostles, 'Brethren, what shall we do?'" (Acts 2:37). If you want to see people respond like that, never change the essential gospel message from group to group. Shifting contexts do not identify reality. Reality is not on the outside; it's on the inside, and all hearts are the same: desperately in need of salvation from sin.

Paul's gospel message never changed from Jew to Gentile. The starting point was often different—for with Jewish people he could start with the common ground of the Old Testament, but with the Gentiles he started with God as creator. But the gospel message itself always remained the same. Paul went from country to country, people group to people group, preaching the same message. That was an era without mass media or globalization; not only were cultures highly defined and restricted, but different societies were also unique at the local, city, town, and even village level. Paul, however, was not paralyzed by any of that; he had no preoccupation with "contextualization." What about 1 Corinthians 9:22: "I have become all things to all men, so that I may by all means save some"? Verse 19 makes clear what he meant: "I have made myself a slave to all, so that I may win more." It wasn't that he changed the gospel message, but that he made any necessary personal sacrifices to preach the gospel to as many people as he could. God help us to be as faithful in our outreach to the lost.

I've seen enough different cultures and preached the gospel in enough contexts and through enough interpreters to know that it is sheer folly to try to change the content of the gospel to suit each one. The gospel isn't our message to adapt. We are ambassadors, tasked with delivering a very simple message accurately. There's nothing more important than getting that message right. It doesn't matter how "cool" you are; what really matters is how *clear* you are in proclaiming God's truth. Wherever I have gone in the world, I have endeavored to preach the same gospel according to Jesus, and God has been faithful to save souls.

Those of us who preach for a living are in the only profession where we can take no credit for what we do—except for what we mess up! We're the only ones in the world responsible for all the failures and none of the successes. Our attitude, therefore, is "all humility and gentleness" (Eph. 4:2). We're never to parade ourselves as if we've accomplished some great thing if God, in his mercy, saves sinners under our preaching. We carry the treasure of the gospel in our lowly selves, likened in Scripture to "earthen vessels, so that the surpassing greatness of the power will be of God and not from ourselves" (2 Cor. 4:7). Remember that the goal of the Christian, well summarized in 1 Corinthians 10:31, is whether "you eat or drink or whatever you do, do all to the glory of God."

CHAPTER 4

IMPROVING THE GOSPEL:

Exercises in Unbiblical Theology (or) Questioning Five Common Deceits

Mark Dever

P eople often try to improve the gospel, but in "improving" it, they always end up losing it. We see this again and again in the New Testament. Some Corinthians, for example, wanted to add human wisdom and eloquence to the gospel. "No harm there," they thought. "That's the kind of communication we are used to, and it will make the gospel culturally appropriate." Some teachers in Galatia wanted to add observance to the ceremonial laws of Moses to the gospel, saying, effectively, that one must become a Jew before trusting in Christ. And teachers in Colossae were adding everything from worldly philosophy to the worship of angels.

Let me give you a simple but possibly revolutionary study suggestion: do a study through the New Testament to find out what the gospel is. Surely we must know this, above all else. Ask the question, "What is included in 'the gospel'?" According to the Bible, God is fundamental to the gospel, as is his creation of us and our plight (that we are lost in sin). Also fundamental is God's solution to that plight in Christ, through his incarnation, substitutionary death, resurrection, and return. Thus Mark begins his gospel, "The beginning of the gospel about Jesus Christ, the Son of God" (1:1).[1] It seems, from 1 Corinthians 15 and 2 Timothy 2:8, that this is what Paul would say is of "first importance." This is his "gospel."

We must also recognize that the command to repent and believe is part of our core message. According to Jesus, instruction in what our response must be is not merely an implication, but rather *part of* the gospel message itself. That is what the risen Christ teaches his disciples in Luke 24:46–47: "This is what is written: The Christ will suffer and rise from the dead on the third day, and repentance and forgiveness of sins will be preached in his name to all nations, beginning at Jerusalem." This is the gospel, as Paul says in Galatians 1:4 of Jesus, "who gave himself for our sins to rescue us from the present evil age, according to the will of our God and Father." We are justified by faith alone in Christ alone—not in ourselves at all. The Spirit of God makes a radical change in us—what the Bible calls "new creation" and "new birth." This is good news, and this central message of the gospel is, and must remain, clear.

New challenges to the clarity and sufficiency of the gospel arise in each generation. Today some people, even within evangelicalism, are acting and speaking as if Jesus Christ alone is not fully sufficient and as if faith in him and his promises alone is a reduction of the full gospel. They are effectively modifying, or expanding, the gospel we have received.

I recently read a column in a leading evangelical magazine in which the author was arguing for our accepting and using the many different presentations of the gospel that we see in Scripture. So, for example, this column said that "Nicodemus and the Samaritan woman received very different messages."[2] Just a few sentences before that he said, "Jesus did not speak the same blanket message to all people." Reading this charitably, I can understand what he means. Obviously Jesus did not use precisely the same words every time he preached the gospel. But that statement could also be easily confused and taken to mean that these differing words are actually differing gospels! I think it would be better to say that there are differing ways to share the same message. You can use different illustrations to explain the incarnation or the atonement, but incarnation and atonement are not mere illustrations to be altered, replaced, or creatively reinterpreted. They are part of the message. Carefully defining the message therefore is not "reductionistic" (as this author warned). Carefully defining the message is, in fact, essential for preserving our hold on it.

Looking more broadly at the rising generation of Christian ministers who profess to believe the gospel, there are several different ways that people are trying to supplement or add to the gospel. Let's consider some of the threats that we face, some of the mistaken notions that threaten to carry us away. These are different threats from those that the New Testament Christians faced, but they are no less undermining of the full sufficiency of the work of Christ. There are many such distortions we could consider, everything from a this-worldly prosperity gospel to a feel-good human potential gospel. I outline below five cries that I think are particularly attractive and threatening to our hold on the gospel.

1) "Make the Gospel Social!"

The question here is, "What did Jesus come to save?" That is, what is the gospel about? This question is all about our mission as Christians. The people who make this cry take our mission to be that of working to save the structures of society as opposed to working to see mere individuals saved. Put another way, the question has to do with how much of the kingdom of God we should expect to see before Christ returns.

Tom Wright, in his book *Surprised by Hope*, says that "the church that takes seriously the fact that Jesus is Lord of all" will "not just seek to order its own life in an appropriate rhythm of worship and work. Such a church will also seek to bring wisdom to the rhythms of work in offices and shops, in local government, in civic holidays, and in the shaping of public life."[3] If what Wright means here is that we ought to educate our members to think biblically about all of life so that they will be equipped to act wisely in all their stewardships, then Wright is certainly right. But if he means that part of the gospel message committed to us is that the church should directly shape the laws of the land, then I do not think there is any such example in the New Testament.

Certainly there is no New Testament example of the church spending time directly instructing the Roman emperor or directly shaping the pagans' view of culture. That may of course be the *effect* of our preaching the gospel and teaching Christians the Word, but we will never by our preaching—or by any of our actions—bring in the culmination of the kingdom of God. That will happen only with the return of Christ. He will, as Revelation 21 shows us so wonderfully, cause his bride to appear. A time will come when all tears are wiped away, but Revelation 21:4 tells us that that is God's action.   Thus, to tell the church to focus primarily on repairing passing structures in a fallen world—a world under the curse of God—would not only cause churches discouragement through the frustration of building sand castles at low tide, but it would, even more horrendously, distract us from the work of bringing God eternal glory by preaching the gospel and seeing people converted and eternally reconciled to God.

Theologically, the question is how much we should identify the kingdom of God with what is going on in this world right now. Some Christians see a complete disjunction, a complete separation of the church from the world, leading them to withdrawal from the world. Partially in response to this error, voices such as Tom Wright's have been raised to champion the biblical witness for God's concern for societal issues such as justice and poverty. But confusion enters when such concern is taken to be either the gospel or the central mission of the local church.

Many talk today of "redeeming the culture" and suggest that some of us have wrongly privatized the gospel. They suggest that the gospel has, as at least one of its goals, the reform of politics and government.[4] In the name of "seeking the peace and the prosperity of the city" (from Jer. 29:7), some pastors are leading churches to take responsibility for local schools, housing developments, and other matters of interest for the wider community. Such good deeds are explained as simply living out Jesus' words in the Sermon on the Mount (Matt. 5:16) and Peter's words about living good lives among the pagans (1 Pet. 2:12). Such ministries are often characterized as the church being "salt and light" (Matt. 5:13–14) and thereby making the church's effect on the surrounding community influential, even irresistibly so. Christians are presented as the vanguard of the new world that God is bringing about—the kingdom—in service of which goal we act in business, education, law, sciences, politics, and the arts.

In the largest sense, the gospel is the good news of God for all of his creation. God's creation was "subjected to frustration" by the fall of man, and has been "groaning" ever since (Rom. 8:19, 22). God will bring this frustration and groaning to an end. Isaiah 61 presents God displaying his splendor by restoring devastated places and renewing ruined cities, by freeing the captives and releasing the prisoners. The whole arc of the Bible presents this as the background, the underlying narrative, of how God is going to display his splendor in creation. Some of the kingdom language in the Gospels refers to this larger hope. But there is a more narrow sense in which this good news is that which informs sinners how we can have a part in this new creation, restored to God's purposes, reconciled to God's person, through the life, death, and resurrection of Jesus Christ. It is in this more narrow sense that the word *gospel* is often used in Scripture, and popularly today. It is an important sense to define carefully and defend vigorously. It is not to be hidden because we consider it too individualistic nor lost by being submerged into the larger sense.[5]

The gospel that has been committed to us is a uniquely Christian message that has been uniquely entrusted to the church. I have non-Christian family and friends that agree with me about the desperate sadness of hunger and malnourishment, unjust governments, or sex-trafficking, and they join me in working to oppose these. But they will not join me in spreading the gospel of Jesus' death for sinners to reconcile us to God. Spiritually, they are at war with this God.

I was once asked by a United States senator if I had any advice for him on a certain matter that had come before the Senate. It was an important matter, an amendment to the United States Constitution, which gave the senator a once-in-a-lifetime kind of vote, although not of the magnitude of issues like slavery or abortion. The House of Representatives had already passed it over-whelmingly, and it looked like it was just about to pass the Senate. Indeed the majority in the Senate were already publicly committed to voting for it, including every other member of the senator's party. But the Constitution requires a super-majority of two-thirds in both the House and the Senate for amendment. The Senate was one vote short for passing it on to the states for ratification.

As it happened, I had strong opinions on the matter, but I couldn't say that Scripture was clear on it. Any comment I might have made likely would have had no influence on the senator anyway. The man is a thoughtful Christian and an experienced public servant. He was probably being kind to me, his pastor, by asking me for my view. But I think that I was being spiritually tempted. I'm not sure what others might have said, but I told the senator that he had his responsibility before God in our political system, as I had mine. I thus declined to comment, saying that I had more important business to attend to with him. I told him that I could be wrong on that amendment, but I was certainly not wrong on the gospel of Jesus Christ.

In Acts 8, Philip preaches "the good news of the kingdom of God and the name of Jesus Christ" (v. 12). The immediate response of his hearers was not to change the structure of the government of their city but to be baptized. Luke reports that from this, the apostles "heard that Samaria had accepted the word of God" (Acts 8:14). It is clear that even using the expression "the good news of the kingdom" does not mean that God's reign has now come in the fullness we will know it in Christ's return. Rather, it means that the king is willing to pardon rebels and that we should *personally* submit ourselves to his rule. Yes, then we will begin to work out the implications of this message, but those implications aren't the gospel itself. If you say such implications *are* part of the gospel, confusion will result. The message of God's fully sufficient work in Christ will be mixed with our own works. There is no entrance into the kingdom apart from personal faith in Jesus Christ.

May the local church be involved in good works? Yes, but it should be as a reflection of and an attraction to this gospel of Jesus Christ. If alleviating material poverty is taken as a responsibility of the congregation because doing so is part of the gospel, then many younger Christians may choose to serve there and not in evangelism. This could well be the choice of less mature Christians, more nominal Christians, those who would rather do things that the world around them recognizes and values instead of the evangelism that the world rejects and scorns. Your congregation may well continue to do both for a season, but I fear that those who follow you will not. Such a social gospel will slowly but surely lose its supernatural awkward corners and be smoothed to be acceptable to sinners all around. It's the story of countless churches in our own land. Walter Rauschenbusch and his early twentieth-century followers are instructive for us here. Evangelism will never be appreciated by the world. It is our special task, pastors, to protect the priority of evangelism.

I don't mean by this to communicate any indifference about issues of this life. Are both evangelism and compassionate service to be part of our individual discipleship? Yes. Are they both to typify our lives as Christians? Yes. Are they equally part of the gospel? No.

A foundation established by evangelical Christians to fund Christian work came, over time, to accept the idea that one cannot preach the gospel without aiming also at other larger, cultural changes. A friend of mine, whose evangelistic ministry those from the foundation had previously known and appreciated, asked for funding to plant a church in a spiritually dark northeastern city. The foundation declined. My friend is deeply concerned with the urban poor and has given himself in caring for many in very practical ways. But he does so simply because he believes that preaching the gospel can be spoken of as the responsibility of the church in a way that social action cannot be. Evangelism must be the priority. So they declined to assist him. That is just one example. Recent history provides example after example of such once-evangelical groups falling away from the priority of the gospel and doing so in ways that directly hinder its being preached.

Never substitute doing good works for sharing the gospel. Don't try to improve the gospel by making it social; you'll end up losing it. We must preach the gospel we have received.

2) "Make the Gospel Larger!"

This cry is similar to the one we have just considered, but it is more common among evangelicals, especially among the Reformed. The question raised here is, "Did Jesus really come *only* to save our souls?" At stake here is what lies at the core of the gospel. What precisely is the gospel? People who make this cry think through a Christian worldview (which is great), and they are seeking to apply the gospel to all of life. But such implications of the gospel are sometimes referred to as *part of* the gospel itself (which is not great). The people I have in mind here would affirm what we mean by "the gospel," but they would want to say more.

Chuck Colson has done some great work; his autobiography helped solidify my own desire for the ministry. He is a man to admire in so many ways. However, he has in this area been confusing, and he serves as an example of what so many ministers today seem to be doing and thinking. Last summer at the Southern Baptist Pastor's Conference, Chuck Colson charged the assembled pastors to "understand what Christianity is," which is an excellent charge to a group of pastors. But then he said, "Christianity is a way of seeing all of life and all of reality, a way of understanding ultimate truth . . . the plan of creation. . . . Christianity is a world view. . . . When Jesus Christ came, he announced the kingdom . . . every aspect of life under the lordship of Christ."

Does that mean that someone who has not thought through the implications of the lordship of Christ is not a Christian? I assume Chuck doesn't mean that. But what does it mean to be a genuine Christian without participating in what he calls "Christianity"? Where is the dividing line between Christian and non-Christian? Is the line found at the place where implications for faith are thought through, or is it simply whether we have faith only in Christ to save us from God's wrath against us because of our sins?

I think there is much at stake in getting this right. The fruit of the Spirit, the transformation of our mind, comes from being a Christian, but it does not effect our salvation. I'm concerned that if we confuse this issue, we might begin to call "Christians" those who have simply tacked fruit on fruitless fruit trees. Non-Christians can hold some of the moral positions Christians hold, but they are not made Christians by holding them. A lack of these moral positions may falsify our claim to be Christians, but no one is made a Christian by holding these positions. It is the gospel that saves and transforms, and the gospel is no collection of our moral positions or actions.

The righting of all wrongs, the blessings mentioned from Isaiah in Jesus' first reading in the synagogue—the releasing of the oppressed, the healing of the blind, the freeing of the prisoners—are taken to be, as Colson has written, "doing the Gospel."[6] I am in favor of thinking through the implications of a Christian worldview, but I am concerned that we not, in the process, misunderstand what a Christian is. We must always be clear to distinguish between the core of the gospel and its results or implications.

Let's consider one implication of the gospel: "Gentiles are heirs together with Israel, members together of one body, and sharers together in the promise in Christ Jesus" (Eph. 3:6). Could this be said to *be* the gospel? It is certainly good news, yet Ephesians 3:6 says this happens through or by the gospel, not that this *is* the gospel. The problem with identifying an effect of the gospel as the gospel itself is the thinking that those who desire and work for that effect are working for the gospel when in fact they may have a very different idea of how that effect comes about—in essence, a very different gospel. Our good deeds commend the gospel only if the gospel has already been verbally communicated. Evangelism is the preaching of the gospel.

Here is another implication: sharing our lives with someone we intend to serve, perhaps even evangelize. But according to Paul in 1 Thessalonians 2:8, that is not sharing the gospel: "We loved you so much that we were delighted to share with you not only the gospel of God but our lives as well." Again, we may wonder if such sharing could be said to *be* the gospel. It certainly is good news. Yet we see that Paul's sharing his life with the Thessalonians was something in addition to sharing the gospel. He could have shared the gospel without sharing his life. We see the problem of confusing an action of ours with the gospel itself, even if that action can be said to reflect the gospel or to be consistent with it, perhaps even be an implication of it. People can share their lives with someone without ever knowing or believing what Paul here means by "the gospel."

When someone says that the gospel includes opposition to abortion or working to end unjust laws, then I have a few questions: does it also include nationalized healthcare or the war in Iraq? Much is lost when an implication of the gospel is bundled together with the gospel, or even called part of the gospel. I understand that it is a rhetorically powerful way for a preacher to make a point of the importance of something, but does it jeopardize the unique message about the reconciling death of Jesus Christ?

Also, what do we say of others who agree with us about Christ but not about particular implications? Can true Christians disagree on how best to care for the poor? Someone may be a supporter of monarchy or of taking away the religious liberties of Baptist preachers, and I disagree with them, but can I say from those sad mistakes that such people could not be my brothers or sisters in Christ, that we could not share the same gospel because we've not worked out the implications in the same way?

For years many of our African-American brothers and sisters have had to listen to us quote favorably writers who believed that racial slavery was morally defensible. I know we don't agree with such defenses, but seminaries have even been named after some who took what we all think were terrible positions. Yet we can say that they understood—and even appreciated—the gospel. We all live imperfectly and inconsistently with what we know to be true. That's why we are saved by faith in Christ alone. To require us to include what we take to be implications of the gospel as part of the gospel itself can too easily confuse our message and cause us to lose the radical and gracious sufficiency of faith in Christ alone. We want a Christian worldview *and* we don't want to confuse that with the gospel.

Don't try to improve the gospel by making it larger; you'll end up losing it. We must preach the gospel we have received.

3) "Make the Gospel Relevant!"

The question here is, "*How* will people be saved?" The concern is with what our outreach should be like; the buzzword is "contextualization." Many writers and pastors seem to begin with the assumption that the gospel appears irrelevant to people today. Therefore, they conclude, we should follow the example of Paul on Mars Hill, or Paul going to Jerusalem and being a Greek to the Greeks or a Jew to the Jews. As Paul said to the Corinthians, he would "become all things to all men so that by all possible means I might save some" (1 Cor. 9:22).

In what can be described as incarnational ministry, we want to figure out what keeps non-Christians from coming to our churches, listening to our sermons, and believing our gospel. As a result, we stress similarities in an attempt to help them feel at home, understood, and cared for when they are among us. We want them to belong so that they will believe. We want to highlight the way the gospel can help them succeed or have purpose or greater joy or some other desired benefit. The more similar we appear to those we are trying to reach, the more the gospel will appear relevant to them, and therefore the more successful we'll be at reaching them. We must beware here. A concern for evangelism, unmoored from the important revealed truth of Scripture, has often been the pathway to theological liberalism. This has always been so, from Schleiermacher in the eighteenth century to Finney in the nineteenth century to the pragmatists in the twentieth century.

In the middle of the last century, a missionary articulated "the homogeneous unit principle." The idea behind it is that like attracts like. We will be more likely to attract unchurched Harry and Mary, or Saddleback Sam, or Indian Brahmins when people who are like them share the gospel with them. One leading proponent of such ideas has written, "Studies have shown that people make a decision for Christ sooner when there is a group support," or, as that same best-selling book advocated, "This is what we want to do with the opening song. We use a bright, upbeat number that makes you want to tap your foot, clap, or at least smile. We want to loosen up the tense muscles of uptight visitors. When your body is relaxed, your attitude is less defensive. . . . If you can reduce visitors' level of fear, they'll be far more receptive to the Gospel."[7] Of course, this kind of thinking will lead us to try to make the gospel relevant to very specific groups of people. So this same book says that the style of music you use in your service "may . . . be the most influential factor in determining who your church reaches for Christ and whether or not your church grows. You must match your music to the kind of people God wants your church to reach."[8]

But such evident relevance to non-Christians brings with it a host of questions. Shouldn't it be our *lives* more than simply our weekly meetings that provoke unbelievers' interest? If we can gain people by lowering their defenses with music and lighting, then couldn't the atheists, Mormons, or Muslims figure out the same kind of marketing manipulation and maybe even do it better? Furthermore, wouldn't such methods display the cleverness of the leaders of that church more than the wisdom of God? I can understand some of this as an evangelistic strategy. It might indeed be good to have soccer players reaching soccer players or members of a retirement community reaching other retirees, but wouldn't we specifically *not* want to build a local congregation around a homogeneous unit?

Paul wrote to the Ephesians, "But now in Christ Jesus you who once were far away have been brought near through the blood of Christ" (2:13). It seems that the overcoming of that ancient barrier actually drew attention to the profound power of the atoning death of Jesus Christ. While there were certainly unique issues in the Jewish/Gentile divide, the worldly divisions that rend our churches seem to suggest that they are more powerful than the gospel of Jesus Christ. If anything, we might say that a *heterogeneous* unit principle is closer to the New Testament understanding of what the gospel accomplishes in our churches.

While Paul certainly did tell the Corinthians that he would "become a Greek to the Greeks or a Jew to the Jews" in order to win people to Christ, it is interesting that earlier in that same letter, Paul had explained how he refused to speak to the Corinthians in the manner that they were accustomed to being spoken to—in human eloquence and wisdom (see 1 Cor. 1–2). It seems that Paul

thought there were some methods which would themselves cause
the message itself to be misunderstood and could perhaps be said
even to contradict the gospel that he would preach to them.

Of course we should contextualize the gospel—and we do so
all the time. You have only to look at where we meet, how we sit,
what language we speak, and how we sing to realize how different
we are in externals from the churches in the book of Acts. And we
should always be willing to follow Christ's example to lay aside our
rights and our preferences in order to serve people with the gospel.
So we learn their language, we go to their country, we eat their
food, and we wear their clothes in so far as we do not contradict
God's revealed will in Scripture. But we do all this not for our own
comfort, nor for the comfort of the sinner in his sin. Any translation work we do should never soften the gospel. Contextualization
should never have as its goal to make the gospel more palatable or
more acceptable to a sinner. In fact, one test of whether a particular
attempt at contextualization has been successful is to ask if it has
made the *offense* of the gospel clearer.

The gospel *is* relevant to every sinner! Our job is merely to
present the gospel accurately, to work to make that already-existing
relevance obvious and clear. If merely human skill works to bring
someone into our church, we can be sure that other greater human
skill will be able to take them out of it. We should reject any kind of
"relevance" that sacrifices the very distinctness that Scripture tells
us will be part of our life-saving witness to the gospel among those
we would reach. We should illustrate the gospel before them by our
lives of Christlike love. Of course we have stupid peculiarities that
may mark us, and we should not be encouraged in those. But we
should have a distinction that bears witness to the very nature and
truth of the gospel. Jesus said, "A new command I give you: Love
one another. As I have loved you, so you must love one another. By
this all men will know that you are my disciples, if you love one
another" (John 13:34–35). So Paul called Christians to shine in the

midst of the dark night of this world. The gospel's relevance appears precisely in our being distinct.

Don't try to improve the gospel by making it more relevant in this way; you'll end up losing it. We must preach the gospel we have received.

4) "Make the Gospel Personal!"

The question here seems to be, "Are we saved alone?" The issue is our identity in Christ. Some people seem to understand the gospel only in reference to themselves as individuals with no idea of the local church. This individualism, which ignores the local church, ends up distorting our discipleship and even our gospel—and this is true for everyone from Harold Camping to George Barna and beyond. After all, what is God about in Jesus Christ? According to Ephesians 3, God's "intent was that now, through the church, the manifold wisdom of God should be made known to the rulers and authorities in the heavenly realms, according to his eternal purpose which he accomplished in Christ Jesus our Lord" (vv. 10–11).

According to the Bible, our participation in the local congregation normally validates or falsifies our claim that we are savingly trusting in Christ and his gospel. What gospel allows you to think you have accepted it, if you don't, in a committed and Christlike way, love your brother? What does saving faith look like? Does the gospel merely save me and lead me to God? Or does it normally bring me to God through the fellowship of the local church? Paul says that "we were all baptized by one Spirit into one body" (1 Cor. 12:13). God means us to serve him not *only*, of course, but *fundamentally* through the local church, where we are served by each other as we administer God's grace to each other by using the gifts God has given us in serving each other (1 Pet. 4:10).

For many today, the Christian life is taken to be something that *they* get to choose to live out as *they* will, with the people *they* want to love—just their family, or just their friends, perhaps gathered around the radio, or the Internet, or on the golf course. I have no doubt that in some places around the world, such fellowship is the only kind of fellowship possible, given how oppressive and tyrannous some governments are. But in many places around the world, we can do what the New Testament Christians seemed to do, as they were able, and gather in larger numbers for fellowship, encouragement, and teaching.

I think most Christians in America only think of the gospel as saving them individually, and thus completely neglect the functional congregation-centeredness that is supposed to mark our discipleship. So many people today are presenting a "gospel" that tells us about Jesus but then leaves us alone or with only a few friends. It is a personal gospel, with something of a designer deity. The idea is that the church is simply one more means that Christians *may* choose to use in order to grow spiritually if they find it helpful, like their choice of music, a Bible study, a devotional book, or a conference. They go to a local church for its lively 9AM service, to another church for its ministry to young married couples, and to yet another church for a mentoring relationship. The idea that they should be fundamentally committed to one congregation and submitted to the leadership there is as foreign to them as eating locusts and wild honey would be to most of us. It's not even so much that they *oppose* the idea; it's just that they simply have never even considered it.

Many evangelicals seem to assume today that *church* is just the plural word for *Christian*, and therefore they assume that the local church should do whatever the individual Christian should do. From this lack of understanding of the church's unique responsibilities and privileges, confusion about the gospel comes. A wrongly personalized gospel winds up with a wrongly personalized "church." Everything the individual Christian has to do becomes then the task of the church. But that can't be true. The church isn't supposed to be the husband of my wife. The church teaches me about being a husband, but I must go and apply it in the intricacies of my unique relationship to my wife. Two different marriages can pursue the same biblical goals in differing ways. How I husband my wife should be guided by the Bible in principle, but my marriage could not be said to be part of the gospel, even though it should be consistent with the gospel and reflect the gospel. We don't have to agree on everything about the Christian life in order to agree about the gospel.

Being vague about the church can hurt our understanding of the gospel. Do we know what God calls us together *for* in the local church? In one popular erroneous view, the church, as the local church, is understood to be a company of Christians with no unique responsibilities. Whether it's a Bible study or a fellowship on a college campus for evangelism or a regular gathering of Christian women in the neighborhood for prayer, many today would consider any of these gatherings a church. But none of these is a local church. Even two or three people gathered together in Jesus' name are not necessarily a church. Such a group is not God's primary plan for displaying his glory to the world. Such a simple identification of any group of Christians as a church tends to make invisible the local church's unique biblical responsibilities for the preaching of the gospel, obedience to baptism and the Lord's Supper, the recognition of elders and submission to them, and defining the membership of the local church, and thus the appearance of the gospel in the world.

Such wrong ideas of the church often encourage wrong ideas of the gospel. Antinomianism is encouraged where there are no people you have to love, and legalism where there are unbiblical standards unchallenged by God's Word rightly preached. The audible gospel is intended to be displayed by the visible local church, full of people who may have little in common except the gospel. The church is not supposed to do everything that is commanded of the individual Christian.

Jesus founded the church, and a local church is supposed to be a

company of Christians joined together, meeting together for fellowship with Christ and each other around his Word and ordinances.
Such a church is intended to be an integral part of a Christian's
life and discipleship. It's not an optional extra. Our life is to be
lived congregationally and in a series not of formal (not informal)
relationships of commitment in which we are accountable to one
another. The local church is a glorious testimony to the gospel,
which is greater than the sum of its visible parts. A local church is
not simply a collection of individual lights; it is a furnace that rages
against the dark that God uses to create more lights.

I love the way Jonathan Edwards presented the centrality of
the church in God's plan: "The creation of the world seems to
have been especially for this end, that the eternal Son of God might
obtain a spouse, towards whom he might fully exercise the infinite
benevolence of his nature, and to whom he might, as it were, open
and pour forth all that immense fountain of condescension, love
and grace that was in his heart, and that in this way God might be
glorified."[9]

Don't try to improve the gospel by decoupling it from the
church; you'll end up losing it. We must preach the gospel we have
received.

5) "Make the Gospel Kinder!"

"*Why* does God save us?" The issue here is God's purpose in salvation. Many people have assumed that the ultimate purpose of the
gospel is the greatest good for the greatest number of people. It
has long been a popular assumption that what God is about in the
gospel is attempting to rescue the most people he can from hell. The
idea is that since God is just and holy as well as loving and merciful, his character is best expressed in providing salvation for sinners
who will take it. Therefore, we should do whatever we can to reach
whomever we can (which in and of itself, of course, is good). But
here, "reaching them" is not seen as merely making sure they hear

and understand the gospel but making sure that they *accept* the gospel. In light of this, all evangelistic efforts are subjected to evaluation according to how many people have heard and have made an immediate, visible positive response. The ultimate purpose of God and the preaching of the gospel is considered to be the salvation of sinners. Period. This, it's thought, is a kinder gospel.

But isn't this really a modification of what Scripture teaches? Could this formulation really owe more to the eighteenth- and nineteenth-century philosophers Jeremy Bentham and John Stuart Mill than to Scripture? Isn't this just the philosophy of utilitarianism in Christian garb? In some ways this problem is the root of the other problems. We come up with a man-centered edition of the gospel in order to make the gospel sound better to unbelieving, non-Christian ears, in order to try to justify God before the bar of the unbelieving world. The results of such attempts litter the history of the church. Brothers, pragmatism is a greater danger for Bible-believing Christians than "open theism" will ever be!

But there is a more *God-centered* gospel where God is chiefly understood not to be about the most sinners saved but about the most glory for himself. Jesus said, "For God so loved the world that he gave his one and only Son, that whoever believes in him shall not perish but have eternal life" (John 3:16). What do you hear when you hear that verse? Do you hear about God and how he has loved us, about what he has done and who he has given, about his giving himself, and about God himself as the object of our faith?

The fruit of pragmatism's change of emphasis—away from God and toward us—inevitably tends to distort creation, as if it's all centered on human ability and faithfulness. After planting the church in Thessalonica, Paul received a good report of the believers there, and he wrote to them, "We always thank God for all of you, mentioning you in our prayers. We continually remember before our God and Father your work produced by faith, your labor prompted by love, and your endurance inspired by hope in our Lord Jesus Christ"

(1 Thess. 1:2–3). Contrast this with what one pastor sent out to his congregation three days after an Easter Sunday service: "Dear Church Family, YOU did it again! By inviting your friends, we had a record Easter. . . . Most important of all, 1,038 of your friends will be spending eternity in heaven because YOU cared enough to invite them to a service!" At the end of his letter he wrote, "What a church family we have!" There wasn't much about God in his letter.

Friends, all that exists does so for God's pleasure. Scripture is clear. God is in this for our salvation—and even our glory, as Paul says in 1 Corinthians 2:7—but also, and more fundamentally, he is in it to please himself, to demonstrate himself to the universe. He has a larger end in mind—the display of his character in his creation, the theater of his splendor. The fruit of God's Spirit in us is meant to confirm us in our faith and to show the truth to the non-Christians around us, even to rulers and authorities in the heavenly realms. Isn't this "unimproved" gospel what we find in Scripture, rather than what we put there?

Our churches are living demonstrations of God's character—his justice and mercy. So Jesus said, "All men will know that you are my disciples, if you love one another," (John 13:35). We have his character stamped on us. We are made by it. His Spirit recreates it in us. That's why Paul instructed the Philippians to "do everything without complaining or arguing, so that you may become blameless and pure, children of God without fault in a crooked and depraved generation, in which you shine like stars in the universe as you hold out the word of life" (Phil. 2:14–16).

Have you ever noticed that this is why God does everything he does? Throughout the book of Ezekiel, again and again, the Lord says that he has done something so that all will know that he is the Lord. According to Ephesians 3:10, God's "intent was that now, through the church, the manifold wisdom of God should be made known to the rulers and authorities in the heavenly realms, according to his eternal purpose which he accomplished in Christ

Jesus our Lord," (Eph. 3:10–11). Do you realize all this is going on in the gospel?

Friends, we should want to see people saved, and for their own good, but even more for God's glory—that the truth about our wonderful God will be known by all. Don't try to improve the gospel by making it appear kinder at first glance. If you do, you'll end up losing the gospel. We must preach the gospel we have received.

Conclusion

Am I just being reductionistic? It may seem so, but I mean to be zealous in recognizing the full sufficiency of Jesus' work for us and our God-given faith in that Savior. This gospel we have received is itself full and lacks nothing. Thus, to add to it is only to detract from it—and from God's glory.

I believe that God cares about issues of justice, and so should we. But that's not the gospel. I believe that we should think through the implications of Scripture's teaching, but that's not the gospel. I believe we must and will make culturally situated decisions about how to approach others with our message, but even those decisions are not the gospel. I believe that salvation fundamentally involves an individual decision, but a genuine response to the gospel will inevitably tie your life up with others, normally in a local church. I believe what the Holy Spirit said through Peter, that God "is patient with you, not wanting anyone to perish, but everyone to come to repentance" (2 Pet. 3:9), but that God in the gospel is also concerned to demonstrate his goodness and justice in both the cross of Christ and the damnation of sinners.

Brothers, guard the gospel. Again and again when Paul summarized the gospel, he talked of Christ's death and resurrection (see 1 Cor. 15:3–8; 2 Tim. 2:8). Sharing creation, fall, redemption, and restoration is great at representing the cosmic flow of the Bible; it is good to know what God is about. But, unless I'm a universalist, I must wonder what that means for me, particularly, if I begin to know myself as a sinner against God. If creation, fall, redemption, and restoration is preached without God, man, Christ, and response, how will anyone know that they are to personally repent and believe?

Rising generation of ministers, hear this call. I don't know how long in God's kindness he will even suffer for such an admonition to be given out to you. The gospel of Jesus Christ is not about temporary structures; it is about immortal beings made in God's image. The gospel of Jesus Christ is not about pressing issues of passing policy; it is about the death of Jesus Christ on the cross once for all time. The gospel of Jesus Christ is not about connecting with the questions the non-Christian has; it is about communicating the answer God has given. The gospel of Jesus Christ is not about me experiencing immediate joy with my friends; it is about my everlasting joy in God, and it leads me into a local church with people as sinful and as inconvenient to love as I am. And the gospel of Jesus Christ is not about the number of sinners saved; it is about the glory of the God who saves anyone at all.

Friends, my goal in all of this is extremely simple. It is to encourage you to keep the gospel clear and free of distortions. Keep the gospel clear. Don't try to improve it.

ADDENDUM:
WHAT IS THE GOSPEL?

Greg Gilbert

There has been much conversation in evangelicalism recently about how Christians should define the gospel—whether we should say that the gospel is purely the message that sinners can be forgiven of sin through repentance and faith in the crucified Christ, or whether it is something broader. The conversation has gotten pointed, if not heated, at times, with those in one camp saying that those in the other camp are being reductionistic about the gospel, and those in that camp retorting that their accusers are actually diluting the gospel and distracting the church from its God-given mission.

It seems to me that we can untangle some of the confusion by making some careful observations. I believe the two major camps in this conversation—those who say the gospel is the good news that God is reconciling sinners to himself through the substitutionary death of Jesus (call them "A") and those who say the gospel is the good news that God is going to renew and remake the whole world through Christ ("B")—are largely talking past one another. In other words, I don't think the A's and the B's are answering the same question.

Of course, both camps say they are answering the question, "What is the gospel?" and thus the tension between the two different answers. But if we pay close attention, I think we'll see that they are actually answering two very different and equally biblical questions. Those two questions are these:

1) What is the gospel? In other words, what is the message a person must believe to be saved?
2) What is the gospel? In other words, what is the whole good news of Christianity?

When an A person hears the question, "What is the gospel?" he understands it to mean, "What is the message a person must believe to be saved?" and he answers it by talking about the death of Christ in the place of sinners and the call to repent and believe. When a B person hears the question, "What is the gospel?" he understands it to mean, "What is the whole good news of Christianity?" and he answers by talking about God's purpose to renew the world through Christ.

You can understand why there would be tension between the two. If you answer the first question by talking about the new creation, people are understandably going to say that your answer is too broad and that you are pushing the cross out of its central place. When people in Scripture asked the question, "What must I do to be saved?" the answer they received was to repent of sin and believe in Jesus—not something about the coming new creation.

Yet it's also true that the Bible sometimes talks about the gospel in terms of the new creation. So to answer the second question by *only* talking about Christ's death in the place of sinners and by saying that everything else is by definition not-gospel (but merely implication of the gospel) is indeed too narrow. That would be to say that promises such as the resurrection of the body, the reconciliation of Jew and Gentile, the new heavens and new earth, and many others are somehow not part of what the Bible holds out as the "good news" of Christianity.

What we need to understand is that neither of these two questions is wrong and neither is more biblical than the other. The Bible asks and answers both of them. Let me show now from Scripture why I think both these questions are legitimate and biblical.

As I read it, the Bible seems to use the word *gospel* in two different but highly related ways. Sometimes it uses *gospel* in a very broad way, that is, to describe *all* the promises that God intends to fulfill in Christ, including not only forgiveness of sin but also everything else that flows from it—the establishment of the kingdom, the new heavens and new earth, etc. There are other times, though, where it uses *gospel* in a very narrow way, that is, to describe *specifically* the forgiveness of sins through the substitutionary death and resurrection of Christ. In those places, the broader promises don't seem to be so much in view.

Here are some of the clearest places, I think, where the Bible uses the word *gospel* in the narrow sense:

1) Acts 10:36-43:[1]

> As for the word that he sent to Israel, preaching good news of peace through Jesus Christ (he is Lord of all), . . . To him all the prophets bear witness that everyone who believes in him receives forgiveness of sins through his name.

Peter says that the gospel he preaches is that of "peace through Jesus Christ," by which he means specifically the good news "that everyone who believes in him receives forgiveness of sins through his name."

2) Romans 1:16-17:

> For I am not ashamed of the gospel, for it is the power of God for salvation to everyone who believes, to the Jew first and also to the Greek. For in it the righteousness of God is revealed from faith for faith, as it is written, "The righteous shall live by faith."

Paul defines the gospel in terms of "salvation" and the righteousness of God being revealed through faith. It becomes clear through the rest of the book that he's talking here about forgiveness of sins (justification) being through faith, not works. His focus in Romans is not on the coming kingdom but on how one becomes a part of it. And that he calls "gospel."

3) 1 Corinthians 1:17–18:

> For Christ did not send me to baptize but to preach the gospel, and not with words of eloquent wisdom, lest the cross of Christ be emptied of its power. For the word of the cross is folly to those who are perishing, but to us who are being saved it is the power of God.

The gospel Paul is sent to preach is "the word of the cross."

4) 1 Corinthians 15:1–5:

> Now I would remind you, brothers, of the gospel I preached to you, which you received, in which you stand, and by which you are being saved, if you hold fast to the word I preached to you—unless you believed in vain. For I delivered to you as of first importance what I also received: that Christ died for our sins in accordance with the Scriptures, that he was buried, that he was raised on the third day in accordance with the Scriptures, and that he appeared to Cephas, then to the twelve.

The gospel Paul preached to them and which they received was that "Christ died for our sins . . . was buried . . . [and] was raised." The continuing references to the appearances shouldn't be taken as part of "the gospel," as if we have to tell someone that Jesus appeared to Peter, the Twelve, and James or we're not telling them the gospel. Those references are meant to establish the resurrection as real and historical.

Now here are some of the clearest places, I think, where it is used in the broad sense:

1) Matthew 4:23:

> And he went throughout all Galilee, teaching in their synagogues and proclaiming the gospel of the kingdom and healing every disease and every affliction among the people.

This is the first mention of the word *gospel* in Matthew's account, so we should expect some contours to be given to the term. To fill in the content of the "gospel of the kingdom" that Jesus preached, we look back to verse 17, the first mention of *kingdom*. There, Jesus is recorded as preaching, "Repent, for the kingdom of heaven is at hand!"

The gospel of the kingdom that Jesus preached was the message that (a) the kingdom had dawned, and (b) those who repent could enter it.

2) Mark 1:14-15:

> Now after John was arrested, Jesus came into Galilee, proclaiming the gospel of God, and saying, "The time is fulfilled, and the kingdom of God is at hand; repent and believe in the gospel."

With the exception of the very first verse, this is the first use of the word in Mark's account. The "gospel of God" that Jesus proclaimed was: "The time is fulfilled, and the kingdom of God is at hand; repent and believe in the gospel."

The gospel of God is the message that (a) the kingdom has dawned, and (b) those who repent and believe can enter it.

3) Luke 4:18:

> The Spirit of the Lord is upon me, because he has anointed me to proclaim good news to the poor. He has sent me to proclaim liberty to the captives and recovering of sight to the blind, to set at liberty those who are oppressed.

This is the Old Testament passage from which Jesus launches his public ministry. The term "good news," as it's used in Isaiah 61, is I think referring to the full-orbed establishment of God's kingdom-rule.

4) Acts 13:32-33:

> And we bring you the good news that what God promised to the fathers, this he has fulfilled to us their children by raising Jesus.

Verse 38 is very clear that the good news Paul brought was that forgiveness of sin comes through "this man." But also in verse 32 the
"good news" is said to be "that what God promised to the fathers,
this he has fulfilled . . . by raising Jesus." Surely God's promises to
the fathers, now fulfilled in Jesus, included but were not limited to
forgiveness of sins?

Looking carefully into the New Testament, it seems to me that the
word *gospel* is used in both a broad way and in a more narrow way.
Broadly, as in Matthew 4, Mark 1, Luke 4, and Acts 13, it refers to all
the promises made to us through the work of Jesus—not only forgiveness of sins, but also resurrection, reconciliation with both God and
others, sanctification, glorification, coming kingdom, new heavens
and new earth, and so forth. You might say that in those cases, "gospel" refers to the whole complex of God's promises secured through
the life and work of Christ. We might call this broader sense the
"gospel of the kingdom." In the narrow sense, such as we see in Acts
10, the whole book of Romans, 1 Corinthians 1, and 1 Corinthians
15, "gospel" refers specifically to the atoning death and resurrection
of Jesus and the call to all people to repent and believe in him. We
might call this narrower sense the "gospel of the cross."

Let me make two other things explicit. First, the broad use of
the word *gospel* necessarily includes the narrow. Look at those
examples from Matthew and Mark. Jesus does not just proclaim the
onset of the kingdom, as many have said. He proclaims the onset
of the kingdom *and* he proclaims the means of entering it. Jesus did
not preach the gospel saying, "The kingdom of heaven has come."
He preached the gospel saying, "The kingdom of heaven has come.
Therefore repent and believe." This is crucial, the difference indeed
between gospel and not-gospel: *to proclaim the inauguration of the
kingdom and the new creation and all the rest* without *proclaiming
how people can enter it—by repenting and being forgiven of their
sins through faith in Christ and his atoning death—is to preach a
non-gospel.* Indeed, it is to preach bad news, since you give people

no hope of being included in that new creation. The gospel of the kingdom is not merely the proclamation of the kingdom. It is the proclamation of the kingdom *together with* the proclamation that people may enter it by repentance and faith in Christ.

Second, it's worth noting explicitly, again, the fact that the New Testament calls the specific, narrow message of forgiveness of sins through Christ "the gospel." Therefore, those who would argue, "If you're just preaching the forgiveness of sins through Christ, and not God's intention to remake the world, you're not preaching the gospel," are wrong. Both Paul and Peter (just to mention names from the above examples) seem quite happy to say that they have preached "the gospel" if they have told people about the forgiveness of sins through the substitutionary death of Jesus, full stop.

If it is true that the New Testament uses the word *gospel* in both a broad and a narrow sense, how are we to understand the relationship between those two senses, between the gospel of the kingdom and the gospel of the cross? That's the next question, and once we answer it, I think it will help us to be clearer in our own minds about some really important questions.

So how do the gospel of the kingdom and the gospel of the cross relate? I already have argued that the gospel of the kingdom *necessarily* includes the gospel of the cross. But more specifically, is the gospel of the cross merely a *part* of the gospel of the kingdom, or something more? Is it central to it, peripheral to it, the heart of it, or something else? And for that matter, why are the New Testament writers willing to apply the word *gospel* to the particular promise of forgiveness of sin through faith in Christ and not to other particular promises that are included in the broad gospel? Why do we never see Paul saying, "And that's my gospel: that humans can be reconciled to each other"?

I think we can get at an answer to all those questions by realizing that the gospel of the cross is not just any part of the gospel of the kingdom. Rather, the gospel of the cross is the gateway, the fountainhead, even the seed, so to speak, of the gospel of the kingdom. Read the whole New Testament, and you quickly realize that its univocal message is that a person cannot *get* to those broad blessings of the kingdom except by being forgiven of sin through the death of Christ. That is the fountain from which all the rest springs.

That, I think, is why it is perfectly appropriate for the biblical authors to call that fountainhead "the gospel" even as they also call the whole package—including forgiveness, justification, resurrection, new creation, and all the rest—"the gospel." Because the broad blessings of the gospel are attained *only* by means of the narrow (atonement, forgiveness, faith, and repentance), and because those blessings are attained *infallibly* by means of the narrow, it's entirely appropriate for the New Testament writers to call that gateway/seed/fountainhead promise "the gospel."

It's also perfectly appropriate for the New Testament to call that fountainhead "the gospel" and at the same time *not* call any other particular blessing of the broader package "the gospel." So we don't call human reconciliation "the gospel." Nor do we even call the new heavens and new earth "the gospel." But we do call forgiveness through atonement "the gospel" because it is the fountainhead of and gateway to all the rest.

There are some important implications that flow from this.

1) It is worth saying again that those who argue that "the gospel" is the declaration of the kingdom are simply wrong. The gospel is not the declaration of the kingdom; it is (in the broad sense) the declaration of the kingdom *together with* the means of entering it.

2) To say that the gospel of the cross is somehow not the gospel, or less than the gospel, is wrong. So long as the question is, "What is the message a person must believe to be saved?" the gospel of the cross *is* the gospel. Jesus, Paul, and Peter say so.

3) To say that the gospel of the kingdom is somehow gospel-plus, or a distraction from the real gospel, is also wrong. So long as the question is, "What is the whole good news of Christianity?"

the gospel of the kingdom is not gospel-plus; it *is* the gospel. Jesus, Paul, and Peter say so.

4) It is wrong to call people Christians simply because they are doing good things and "following Jesus' example." To be a Christian, to be a partaker of the blessings of the kingdom, requires one first to go through the gate—that is, to come to Christ in faith and to be forgiven of sin and atoned for. Bunyan tells the story in *The Pilgrim's Progress* about the characters Mr. Formalist and Mr. Hypocrisy whom Christian meets on the path to the Celestial City. After a moment's conversation, however, Christian realizes that they had jumped the wall to the path rather than going through the Wicket Gate. These two are not Christians, regardless of how well they are now navigating the path. To change the characters a bit, there are many people out there who must realize that Mr. Jesus-Follower and Mrs. Kingdom-Life-Liver are *not* Christians—not unless they have come to the crucified Jesus in repentance and faith for the forgiveness of their sins. A person can "live like Jesus lived" all he wants to, but unless he goes through the Wicket Gate of atonement, faith, and repentance, he has not really come to Christ. He has simply jumped the wall.

5) I believe it is wrong ever to say that non-Christians are doing "kingdom work." A non-Christian working for human reconciliation or justice is doing a good thing, but that is not kingdom work, because it is not done in the name of the King. C. S. Lewis was wrong; you cannot do good things in the name of Tash and expect Aslan to be happy about it.

6) The ultimate goal of any mercy ministry—whether done by an individual Christian or a church—has to be to point the world back to the gate. Much could be said here, but I think understanding all this rightly can provide a powerful missionary motive and a penetrating witness to the world. When you renovate a barbershop in the name of Jesus, for instance, you need to tell the owner (to put it sharply for brevity's sake), "Look, I'm doing this because I serve a God who cares about things like beauty and order and peace. In

fact, the Bible says and I believe that God is one day going to recreate this world and inaugurate a kingdom where paint won't peel and trees won't die. But [and here we get to the point] unless you repent and believe in Christ, *I don't think you're going to be a part of that because of your sin.*" And then you tell him the good news of the cross. If you just renovate the barber shop and proclaim the coming kingdom, you've fallen short of proclaiming the gospel. The gospel of the kingdom is the declaration of the kingdom *together with* the means of getting into it.

7) As I've argued before, I believe that many in the so-called emergent church—for all their insistence about how astonishing and surprising their gospel is—have missed entirely what really *is* astonishing about the gospel. That Jesus is king and has inaugurated a kingdom of love and compassion is not really all that astonishing. Every Jew knew that was going to happen someday. What is truly astonishing about the gospel is that the messianic King *dies* to save his people—that the divine Son of Man in Daniel, the Davidic Messiah, and the suffering servant in Isaiah turn out to be the same man. That, moreover, is ultimately how we tie together the gospel of the kingdom and the gospel of the cross. Jesus is not just King, but crucified King. Next to that, what many in the emergent church are holding out as an astonishing gospel is not astonishing at all. It's just boring.

8) Everything we've said so far drives toward the conclusion that evangelistic, missiological, and pastoral emphasis in this age belongs on the gospel of the cross—on the fountainhead, the gateway of the broader gospel of the kingdom. That is because all the rest is unattainable and indeed *bad* news unless we point people there. Not only so, but this is the age in which God's overarching command to every human in the world is "repent and believe." There is only one command that is actually included in the gospel itself (whether broad or narrow): repent and believe. That is the primary obligation on human beings in this age, and therefore it must be our primary emphasis in our preaching, too.

CHAPTER 5

THE CURSE MOTIF OF THE ATONEMENT

R. C. Sproul

For all who rely on works of the law are under a curse; for it is written, "Cursed be everyone who does not abide by all things written in the Book of the Law, and do them." Now it is evident that no one is justified before God by the law, for "The righteous shall live by faith." But the law is not of faith, rather "The one who does them shall live by them." Christ redeemed us from the curse of the law by becoming a curse for us—for it is written, "Cursed is everyone who is hanged on a tree"—so that in Christ Jesus the blessing of Abraham might come to the Gentiles, so that we might receive the promised Spirit through faith.

GALATIANS 3:10–14[1]

For over fifty years I have studied and read a host of tomes written about the meaning of the cross of Christ, and yet I still believe that I have not been able to do anything more than touch the surface of the depths and the riches that are contained in that moment of redemptive history. I suspect that when my eyes open in heaven for the first time, I will be absolutely staggered by the sudden increase of understanding that will come to me when I behold the Lamb who was slain and hear angels and archangels singing in my ears,

"Worthy is the Lamb who was slain, to receive power and wealth and wisdom and might and honor and glory and blessing" (Rev. 5:12), and when I see the apostle Paul and say, "Thank you for knowing nothing but Christ and him crucified."

When we go to the New Testament and read not only the narrative event of the cross but the many didactic expressions that explain to us its meaning and significance, I think we are soon aware that there is no one image or dimension that can comprehensively explain the cross. Rather, we find many images and metaphors that would indicate that the cross is a multifaceted event. It is by no means one-dimensional. It is as a magnificent tapestry woven by several distinct brightly hued threads that, when brought together, give us a magnificent finished work of art.

When the New Testament speaks of the atonement of Jesus, it does so in terms of substitution; it calls attention to a death that in some way was vicarious. The New Testament speaks of the satisfaction of the justice and wrath of God. In Scripture we see the metaphor of the kinsman redeemer who paid the bridal price to purchase his bride with his blood, releasing her from bondage. We see that motif used in the New Testament when it speaks of ransom that is paid. We find the motif of victory over Satan and the powers of darkness when the serpent's head is crushed under the bruised heel of the Redeemer.

But one image, one aspect, of the atonement has receded in our day almost into obscurity. We have been made aware of present-day attempts to preach a more gentle and kind gospel. In our effort to communicate the work of Christ more kindly we flee from any mention of a curse inflicted by God upon his Son. We shrink in horror from the words of the prophet Isaiah (chap. 53) that describe the ministry of the suffering servant of Israel and tells us that it pleased the Lord to bruise him. Can you take that in? Somehow the Father took pleasure in bruising the Son when he set before him that awful cup of divine wrath. How could the Father be pleased by bruising his Son were it not for his eternal purpose through that bruising to restore us as his children?

But there is the curse motif that seems utterly foreign to us, particularly in this time in history. When we speak today of the idea of curse, what do we think of? We think perhaps of a voodoo witch doctor that places pins in a doll made to replicate his enemy. We think of an occultist who is involved in witchcraft, putting spells and hexes upon people. The very word *curse* in our culture suggests some kind of superstition, but in biblical categories there is nothing superstitious about it.

Blessings and Curses in Biblical History

The idea of the curse is deeply rooted in biblical history. We need only to go to the opening chapters of Genesis to the record of the fall of man, the event that provoked from God his anathema on the serpent, who was cursed to go around on his belly. The curse was then given to the earth itself: it would bring forth thorns and briars, making it difficult for Adam to live by the toil of his brow. The curse also brought excruciating (I choose that word carefully) pain to women during childbirth.

But not only do we find this idea of curse early in Genesis, but if we fast-forward to the giving of the law under Moses, we see that God attached to the covenant he made with his people at Sinai a positive sanction and a negative sanction. The positive sanction is articulated there in terms of the concept of blessedness:

> If you faithfully obey the voice of the LORD your God, being careful to do all his commandments that I command you today, the LORD your God will set you high above all the nations of the earth. And all these blessings shall come upon you and overtake you, if you obey the voice of the LORD your God. Blessed shall you be in the city, and blessed shall you be in the field. Blessed shall be the fruit of your womb and the fruit of your ground and the fruit of your cattle, the increase of your herds and the young

of your flock. Blessed shall be your basket and your kneading bowl. Blessed shall you be when you come in, and blessed shall you be when you go out. (Deut. 28:1–6)

God adds that if his people keep his Word, he will bless them—in the city and the country, when they rise up and lie down. God will bless them in the kitchen, the bedroom, and the living room. He will bless their fields, their goats, their sheep, and their cows. If they keep his Word, their lives will be nothing but an experience of divine benediction and blessedness. But God goes on to say:

If you will not obey the voice of the LORD your God or to be careful to do all his commandments and his statues that I command you today, then all these curses shall come upon you and overtake you. Cursed shall you be in the city, and cursed shall you be in the field. Cursed shall be your basket and your kneading bowl. Cursed shall be the fruit of your womb and the fruit of your ground, the increase of your herds and the young of your flock. Cursed shall you be when you come in, and cursed shall you be when you go out. (vv. 15–19)

In the kitchen, in the living room, in the bedroom, in the garage—cursed.

One of the things I love about Christmas is the singing of carols. One of my favorites is "Joy to the World":

No more let sins and sorrows grow,
Nor thorns infest the ground;
He comes to make His blessings flow
Far as the curse is found,
Far as the curse is found,
Far as, far as, the curse is found.

How far do we find that curse? The apostle Paul says that the whole creation groans together in travail waiting for the manifestation of the sons of God. We live on a planet that is under the curse of God. I'd like to take some time to explore the significance of God's divine curse.

Oracles of Weal and Woe

When the prophets of the Old Testament spoke—not their opinions but the word that God placed in their mouths—the favorite method the prophets used to express the word of God was the oracle. It seems that sometimes the only place we see the concept of the oracle is in Greek mythology, such as in the Oracle of Delphi, where we find people going to self-appointed prophets to get a divine pronouncement. Well, there were oracles before Delphi—there was one called Isaiah and others called Jeremiah, Amos, Hosea, Ezekiel, and Daniel. They used the oracular form to communicate the Word of God.

There were two basic kinds of oracles known to the prophets. There was the oracle of weal, which was an oracle of good news, an announcement of prosperity coming from the hand of God, and there was the oracle of woe, an announcement of doom also coming from the hand of God. The oracle of weal was typically uttered by the use of the term *blessed*, the pronouncement of a divine benediction.

David begins the Psalms:

Blessed is the man
    who walks not in the counsel of the wicked,
nor stands in the way of sinners,
    nor sits in the seat of scoffers;
but his delight is in the law of the LORD,
    and on his law he meditates day and night.

He is like a tree
    planted by streams of water
that yields its fruit in its season,
    and its leaf does not wither.

> *In all that he does, he prospers.*
> *The wicked are not so,*
> > *but are like chaff that the wind drives away. (Ps. 1:1–4)*

How often did our Lord exercise the function of the prophet and make oracular pronouncements such as he did on the Sermon on the Mount? There he looked to his disciples and said, "Blessed are the poor. . . . Blessed are those who mourn. . . . Blessed are the meek. . . . Blessed are those who hunger and thirst for righteousness. . . . Blessed are the pure in heart. . . . Blessed are the peacemakers. . . . Blessed are those who are persecuted for righteousness' sake" (Matt. 5:3–10). We call that section of the sermon "the Beatitudes" because Jesus pronounces the blessing of God upon certain people.

The oracle of doom, in contrast, was normally prefaced by the word *woe*. When Amos pronounced the judgments of God on the nations he said, "Woe to you who desire the day of the LORD! . . . Woe to those who are at ease in Zion. . . . Woe to those who lie on beds of ivory" (Amos 5:18; 6:1, 4). When Isaiah beheld the unveiled holiness of God, he pronounced an oracle of doom upon himself because he understood God (Isa. 6:5).

We love to hear the story of blessedness, but we never want to hear the woe. Besides ours, I don't think there has been a culture in the history of the world that has experienced more discontinuity at that level. Everywhere in America we see automobiles with bumper stickers that read *God Bless America*. After 9/11 Pat Robertson and Jerry Falwell suggested that perhaps the events of that day were God's judgments upon America, and the outrage of the press was so severe they had to recant their musings on that point. We believe in a God who is infinitely capable of blessing people but is utterly incapable of cursing them. When I was a young Christian, I heard a sermon from Billy Graham in which he said, "If God does not judge America, he's going to have to apologize to Sodom and Gomorrah." But the idea of God bringing judgment and wrath and curse upon a nation has been expurgated from our Bibles and from our theologies.

The Hebrew Benediction

If you really want to understand what it meant to a Jew to be cursed, I think the simplest way is to look at the famous Hebrew benediction in the Old Testament, one which clergy often use as the concluding benediction in a church service:

> The LORD *bless you and keep you;*
> *the* LORD *make his face to shine upon you and be gracious to you;*
> *the* LORD *lift up his countenance upon you and give you peace.*
>   *(Num. 6:24–26)*

The structure of that famous benediction follows a common Hebrew poetic form known as parallelism. There are various types of parallelism in Hebrew literature. There's antithetical parallelism in which ideas are set in contrast one to another. There is synthetic parallelism, which contains a building crescendo of ideas. But one of the most common forms of parallelism is synonymous parallelism, and, as the words suggest, this type restates something with different words. There is no clearer example of synonymous parallelism anywhere in Scripture than in the benediction in Numbers 6, where exactly the same thing is said in three different ways. If you don't understand one line of it, then look to the next one, and maybe it will reveal to you the meaning.

We see in the benediction three stanzas with two elements in each one: "bless" and "keep"; "face shine" and "be gracious"; and "lift up the light of his countenance" and "give you peace." For the Jew, to be blessed by God was to be bathed in the refulgent glory that emanates from his face. "The Lord bless you" means "the Lord make his face to shine upon you." Is this not what Moses begged for on the mountain when he asked to see God? Yet God told him that no man can see him and live. So God carved out a niche in the rock and placed Moses in the cleft of it, and God allowed Moses to see a glimpse of his backward parts but not of his face. After Moses had gotten that brief glance of the back side of God, his face shone for an extended period of time. But what the Jew longed for was to see God's face, just once.

The Jews' ultimate hope was the same hope that is given to us in the New Testament, the final eschatological hope of the beatific vision: "Beloved, we are God's children now, and what we will be has not yet appeared; but we know that when he appears we shall be like him, because we shall see him as he is" (1 John 3:2). Don't you want to see him? The hardest thing about being a Christian is serving a God you have never seen, which is why the Jew asked for that.

There is a scene in the movie *Ben Hur* where Ben has been reduced to slavery and is being dragged behind his captor. They finally come to a well in the midst of the desert. Ben's lips are parched and he is overcome with thirst. All of a sudden we see someone come out of the shadows, and he stoops over and gives Ben a cup of cold water. The camera is positioned to reflect Ben Hur's vision. As he looks up into the face of the one giving him the water, Ben's face begins to shine. The viewer doesn't have to be told who gave him the drink of water; it is understood that the Lord Jesus made his face to shine upon this slave.

But my purpose here is not to explain the blessing of God but its polar opposite, its antithesis, which again can be seen in vivid contrast to the benediction. The supreme malediction would read something like this: "May the Lord curse you and abandon you. May the Lord keep you in darkness and give you only judgment without grace. May the Lord turn his back upon you and remove his peace from you forever."

The Core of the Gospel

There are several animals involved in the ritual performed on the Day of Atonement. Before the high priest can enter into the Most

Holy Place (which he alone can do only one day each year), he must make a blood sacrifice and go through an elaborate process of purification. There are two more animals involved, one that is killed and another that survives. The one that is killed yields blood, which the high priest takes into the inner sanctum and sprinkles on the mercy seat to bring reconciliation. Yet, in this drama there is no power in that blood other than its pointing forward to the blood of the Lamb, even as the blood on the doorposts on the night of Passover pointed beyond itself to Christ.

We know two things from the Day of Atonement. First, that without the shedding of blood there is no forgiveness of sins. We also learn from the author of Hebrews that the blood of bulls and goats cannot take away sin. But in the drama of the blood sacrifice that is sprinkled on the mercy seat, an act of propitiation is symbolized, which some brilliant translators in the middle of the twentieth century decided to take out of the New Testament, to their everlasting shame.

Those are two words at the core of the gospel—*propitiation* and *expiation*. They have the same root but different prefixes. People must understand propitiation and expiation if they are going to understand the gospel. I use the structure of my church, St. Andrew's, as an illustration. The church is built in a classical style called the cruciform. If it is viewed from the air, the shape of our building forms a cross. Those who walk down the center aisle are reminded of the vertical piece of the cross. I tell my congregation to let it remind them of propitiation. In propitiation the Son does something to satisfy the justice and the wrath of the Father. It is a vertical translation, which was prefigured in the sacrifice made on the mercy seat.

Let's not forget the other animal that liberal theologians try every which way to erase from the biblical record. I'm speaking of the goat, the scapegoat, which became the object of imputation when the priest lay his hands on the back of the animal, symbolically indicating the transfer of the guilt of the people to the back of the goat. Afterward the goat was driven into the wilderness, outside the camp. In the middle of the camp, equidistant to every settlement of every tribe, was the tabernacle, which indicated that God was in the midst of his people. So to be driven out of camp, outside the covenant community, was to be driven to the place where the blessings of God did not reach. That's what Christ did for us in expiation.

When on the cross, not only was the Father's justice satisfied by the atoning work of the Son, but in bearing our sins the Lamb of God removed our sins from us as far as the east is from the west. He did it by being cursed. "Christ redeemed us from the curse of the law by becoming a curse for us—for it is written, 'Cursed is everyone who is hanged on a tree'" (Gal. 3:13). He who is the incarnation of the glory of God became the very incarnation of the divine curse.

Many years ago I was asked by the Quaker community of Pennsylvania, the Society of Friends, to come to one of their meetings and explain to them the difference between the old covenant and the new covenant. I talked about the Day of Atonement in Israel and the crucifixion of Christ in the New Testament. As I spoke of Christ becoming cursed, my message was interrupted by a guy in the back who stood up and shouted, "That's primitive and obscene!" I was taken aback, and just to give myself a chance to think I said, "What did you say?" as if I hadn't heard him. (Everybody in the room heard him.)

With great hostility he repeated himself, so I told him that I loved the words he'd chosen. What could be more primitive than killing animals and placing the blood over the throne of God or taking a human being and pouring out his blood as a human sacrifice? One of the things I love about the gospel is that it wasn't written merely for an agnostic elite group of scholars. The drama of redemption is communicated in terms so simple, so crass and primitive, that a child can understand it. I really like the second word he used—obscene. If there ever was an obscenity that violates contemporary community standards, it was Jesus on the cross. After he became the scapegoat and the Father had imputed to him every sin of every one of his people, the most intense, dense concentration of evil ever experienced on this planet was exhibited. Jesus was the ultimate obscenity.

So what happened? God is too holy to look at sin. He could not bear to look at that concentrated monumental condensation of evil, so he averted his eyes from his Son. The light of his countenance was turned off. All blessedness was removed from his Son, whom he loved, and in its place was the full measure of the divine curse.

All the imagery that betrays the historical event of the cross is the imagery of the curse. It was necessary for the Scriptures to be fulfilled that Jesus not be crucified by Jews; he had to be delivered into the hands of the Gentiles. He had to be executed not by stoning but by Gentiles outside the camp so that the full measure of the curse and the darkness that attends it be visited upon Jesus.

Forsaken

God adds to these details astronomical perturbations. At midday he turned the lights out on the hill outside of Jerusalem so that when his face moved away, when the light of his countenance shut down, even the sun couldn't shine on Calvary. Bearing the full measure of the curse, Christ screamed, "Eli, Eli lema sabachthani," that is, "My God, my God, why have you forsaken me?" (Matt. 27:46).

Jesus took that occasion to identify with the psalmist in Psalm 22 in order to call attention to those looking upon the spectacle that what they were witnessing was really a fulfillment of prophecy. I don't think Jesus was in a Bible-quoting mood at the time. His cry was not, as Albert Schweitzer opined, the cry of a disillusioned prophet who had believed that God was going to rescue him at the eleventh hour and then felt forsaken. He didn't just feel forsaken;

he was forsaken. For Jesus to become the curse, he had to be completely forsaken by the Father.

As I said, I've been thinking about these things for fifty years,
and I can't begin to penetrate all it meant for Jesus to be forsaken by
God. But there is none of that to be found in the pseudo-gospels of
our day. Every time I hear a preacher tell his people that God loves
them unconditionally, I want to ask that the man be defrocked for
such a violation of the Word of God. What pagan does not hear in
that statement that he has no need of repentance, so he can continue
in sin without fear, knowing that it's all taken care of? There is a
profound sense in which God does love people even in their corruption, but they are still under his anathema.

The Gospel—Our Only Hope

Just because a man is ordained is no guarantee that he is in the
kingdom of God. The odds are astronomical that many are still
under the curse of God. There are ordained men who have not yet
fled to the cross, who are still counting on the nebulous idea of the
unconditional love of God to get them through, or even worse, still
thinking that they can get into the kingdom of God through their
good works. They don't understand that unless they perfectly obey
the law of God, which they have not done for five minutes since they
were born, they are under the curse of God. That is the reality we
must make clear to our people—either they will bear the curse of
God themselves or they will flee to the One who took it for them.

Thomas Aquinas once was asked whether he thought that Jesus
enjoyed the beatific vision throughout his whole life. Thomas said,
"I don't know, but I'm sure that our Lord was able to see things
that our sin keeps us from seeing." Remember that the promise of
the vision of God in the Beatitudes is the promise made to the pure
of heart. The reason why we can't see God with our eyes is not that
we have a problem with our optic nerve. What prevents us from
seeing God is our heart, our impurity. But Jesus had no impurity. So

obviously he had some experience of the beauty of the Father until that moment that our sin was placed upon him, and the One who was pure was pure no more, and God cursed him.

It was as if there was a cry from heaven, as if Jesus heard the words "God damn you," because that's what it meant to be cursed and under the anathema of the Father. I don't understand that, but I know that it's true. I know that every person who has not been covered by the righteousness of Christ draws every breath under the curse of God. If you believe that, you will stop adding to the gospel and start preaching it with clarity and boldness, because, dear friends, it is the only hope we have, and it is hope enough.

CHAPTER 6

WHY THEY HATE IT SO:

The Denial of Substitutionary Atonement in Recent Theology

R. Albert Mohler Jr.

In 1739, Charles Wesley read and reflected on Acts 16:26: "Suddenly there was a great earthquake, so that the foundations of the prison were shaken. And immediately all the doors were opened, and everyone's bonds were unfastened." Responding to the passage as only Wesley could do, he sat down and wrote a hymn we have learned to cherish, "And Can It Be?" The hymn is a celebration of the substitutionary atonement of the Lord Jesus Christ, a personal testimony of praise for a sacrificial Savior.

> And can it be that I should gain an interest in the Savior's blood?
> Died He for me, who caused His pain—for me, who Him to
>   death pursued?
> Amazing love! How can it be, that Thou, my God, shouldst die
>   for me?
>
> He left His Father's throne above, so free, so infinite His grace—
> Emptied Himself of all but love, and bled for Adam's
>   helpless race:
> 'Tis mercy all, immense and free, for O my God, it found
>   out me!

Long my imprisoned spirit lay, fast bound in sin and nature's night;
Thine eye diffused a quickening ray—I woke, the dungeon
    flamed with light;
My chains fell off, my heart was free, I rose, went forth,
    and followed Thee.

No condemnation now I dread; Jesus, and all in Him, is mine;
Alive in Him, my living Head, and clothed in righteousness divine,
Bold I approach th'eternal throne, and claim the crown, through
Christ my own.

This lyrical gem of systematic theology, a personal narrative containing propositional truth, is sung in churches around the world. The hymn proclaims the gospel, a gospel that is not mere abstract truth or subjective feeling. Rather, we sing these words in the first person singular—"*me*, who Him to death pursued"; "And can it be that *I* should gain an interest in the Savior's blood?" We cherish these lines precisely because they express our own testimony of faith in Christ. However, as beloved as these lyrics are to us, we quickly discover that this love is not shared by everyone. We must recognize that some people recoil in horror from these words, despising the image they invoke and rejecting the truth they proclaim.

At the beginning of each academic semester I have the privilege of leading The Southern Baptist Theological Seminary community in singing our very own seminary hymn, "Soldiers of Christ in Truth Arrayed." Written by Basil Manly Jr. for our first commencement service in 1859, it has been sung at every commencement since. The first line reads:

Soldiers of Christ in truth arrayed, a world in ruins need your aid:
A world, by sin, destroyed and dead; a world for which the Savior
bled.

Although these lines served us well in our worship for over a century, during the 1970s the word "bled" was changed to "died"—

"A world for which the Savior died." Gone was the reference to the blood.

In the early 1990s, around the same time I became president of the seminary, the Southern Baptist Convention published a new hymnal. They included this hymn, but they changed the word back from "died" to "bled." I was pleased. Shortly thereafter, a faculty member of more liberal days told me that he too was pleased with the change. I was surprised he was pleased, but I was pleased that he was pleased. Unfortunately, he continued talking, and my pleasure fell away as he said, "I'm so glad they changed that back because the word *died* made for such awful poetry. *Died* did not rhyme with *dead*." Awful poetry? Sure, but poor rhyme schemes do not equal a theological tragedy. The true scandal occurs when professing Christians find embarrassment in using words like "bled" or "blood" when referring to the atoning work of Jesus Christ.

The seminary I lead has been through a process of theological transformation. Our seminary and the churches to which we belong must sing a testimonial word of praise similar to "And Can It Be?" for our institutional recovery came only by God's grace and mercy. I am often asked why the change was necessary. My answer to that question is necessarily autobiographical, for I was once a student at the seminary, and I saw firsthand the magnitude of the problem.

The trouble emerged even on the very first day of my studies, in the very first class, in the very first hour. The professor introduced the syllabus, and then he asked each of us to state our name and where we were from and to give the reason why we were taking this course in New Testament studies. As each student answered, chair to chair and desk to desk, it finally came to a young woman who was studying to be an international missionary. She gave her name and home state, and then she said, "I am taking this course because I want to know more about Jesus Christ and his shed blood."

The professor exploded. He said, "There will be no more bloody cross religion in this classroom!" I was unprepared for this. The class was unprepared for this. He continued, "This is not to be tolerated. It is beneath dignity and self-respect to believe in a God who had to kill in order to forgive. Is this understood?" I don't know if everyone in the class that day understood where the professor was coming from, but we definitely understood where the professor would not allow our discussion to head.

Resistance to any mention of the blood of Christ, to the wrath of God, or to a penal substitutionary atonement—these hostilities are all around us. But I want to note that when we ask the question, "Why do they hate it so?" the focus of my concern is not why the unregenerate hate the atonement. Such hostility from non-Christians should not surprise us. The real question of concern is, "Why would some who at least claim to be Christian hate it so?"

Substitutionary Atonement under Attack

Although controversy over the atonement has been alive throughout the centuries of church history, certain milestones have been established in more recent years. On May 21, 1922, Harry Emerson Fosdick, then preacher at the First Presbyterian Church of New York City, rose to deliver the most famous sermon of his entire career, "Shall the Fundamentalists Win?" In the sermon, Fosdick complained that fundamentalists sought to define Christianity in terms of certain definite doctrines and doctrinal boundaries. Fosdick, a self-conscious liberal, rejected many of these doctrines even as he still desired the title of "evangelical." He said this:

> It is interesting to note where the Fundamentalists are driving in their stakes to mark out the deadline of doctrine around the church, across which no one is to pass except on terms of agreement. They insist that we must all believe in the historicity of certain special miracles, preeminently the virgin birth of our Lord, that we must believe in a special theory of inspiration; that the original documents of scripture, which of course we no longer possess, were inerrantly dictated to men a good deal as a man

might dictate to a stenographer; that we must believe in a special theory of the Atonement—that the blood of our Lord, shed in a substitutionary death, placates an alienated Deity and makes possible welcome for the returning sinner.[1]

Fosdick's sermon reveals that in 1922, at least, it was well understood that the doctrine of the atonement found virtually no opposition within any movement legitimately defined as evangelical. Opposition to the doctrine came only from outside evangelicalism. Men like Fosdick complained that those who were within more conservative and orthodox circles made this doctrine of substitutionary atonement a dividing line.

As recently as the 1970s, J. I. Packer described penal substitutionary atonement as "a distinguishing mark of the worldwide evangelical fraternity."[2] Packer wrote that sentence with confidence. Later, in another essay, Packer states that for the entirety of his ministry, the doctrine of substitutionary atonement has been controversial. It is clear from the context of Packer's statement that he described the controversy as being something found in the larger theological world. But now, the controversy has arrived within evangelical circles.[3]

Antipathy to the idea of a penal substitutionary atonement presents itself in such blatant form that it is impossible not to get the point. For example, in November of 1993 a conference was held in Minneapolis entitled "Re-imagining God." At that conference, Professor Delores S. Williams of Union Theological Seminary in New York City said, "I don't think we need a theory of atonement at all. I don't think we need folks hanging on crosses and blood dripping and weird stuff."[4] Williams argued that the Christian church should reject and dispense with any doctrine of atonement. Clearly, she does not believe in sin, at least not in categories that are even remotely biblical. She refuses to believe in a holy and just God who requires a penalty for sin. Williams says, "Forgiveness does not come through blood sacrifice, but through compassion and solidarity."[5] At another conference shortly thereafter, she asked this question: "How do we stay in relationship with those who still find meaning in the blood?"[6]

Substitutionary Atonement and the Theological Framework

It is important to place the doctrine of the atonement into the framework of the larger project of theology—an understanding of the work of Christ, the meaning of his work, and the means of its appropriation. It is important to realize that when we consider the atonement, we are thinking generally in terms of two great categories, the objective and the subjective.

Objective understandings of the atonement center on the fact that God's disposition towards sinners must change. Something objective must take place, a change in how God looks to humanity, to those who are covered by the blood of Christ. In contrast, subjective understandings of the atonement center on the sinner's disposition toward God. That which must change is internal to the sinner. In order to be more accepting of the God who would send or who would allow Christ to die upon the cross, the sinner must change his understanding of God.

In considering the entire presentation of biblical theology, we must recognize that there is, to some extent, a false dichotomy between the objective and the subjective understandings of the atonement. That is, if you believe in the objective aspects of the atonement, then you also believe in its subjective appropriation, in the experience of the one who comes to faith in Christ. However, there can be nothing meaningful to the subjective understanding if it is not first grounded in the prior objective reality of the atonement achieved by Christ.

To understand the reality of what God was doing through the substitutionary sacrifice of his Son is to come face-to-face with the wonder of God's love, mercy, holiness, and grace. There is no way that the atonement can be understood as an objective act without the believer being transformed by this knowledge.

The sum and substance of the gospel is that a holy and righteous God who must demand a full penalty for our sin both *demands* the penalty and *provides* the penalty. His own self-substitution is Jesus Christ the Son, whose perfect obedience and perfectly accomplished atonement purchased all that is necessary for our salvation. Jesus Christ met the full demands of the righteousness and justice of God against our sin. We either believe that or we do not.

If we do not believe this, then our gospel can be nothing more than some kind of message intended to reach an emotive level so that humans will think better of God and might want to associate with him. Or we could transform all these theological categories into merely therapeutic terms and argue that the point of the atonement is for people with problems to realize that there are psychological resources for the repair of their troubled souls. Or we could put forth a merely political atonement, proposing that the gospel sends some kind of signal, both to God's people (as they would define themselves) and to the larger world.

However, if we desire to remain faithful to the biblical text, we will believe and teach that the central thrust of the atonement is that God demanded a punishment for sin and requires atonement by his holiness and justice. We also will believe and teach that God provided this necessary atonement through Jesus Christ, who died on our behalf, paying in full the penalty for our sin, not only associating himself with our sin, but becoming sin for us "who knew no sin, so that in him we might become the righteousness of God" (2 Cor. 5:21).[7]

The atonement is subjectively experienced by the believer through redemption and through union with Jesus Christ. We understand that this atonement is divinely applied by the Holy Spirit, who convicts the soul of sin, opens and quickens the eyes of the soul to see and to believe, and then sets his seal upon the believer. We must be on the lookout for the growing resistance to the idea that the objective dimension of the atonement is unnecessary, or even contrary, to God's gracious character. Nothing less than the gospel is at stake.

If we were to try to exhaust all the different metaphors and models of atonement, not only in the Scripture but also in classical orthodox Christian theology, the task would be far beyond the limitations of this essay. But it is important to see that there are at least three clusters of understandings that have been presented through the history of the church. J. I. Packer suggests there are three main accounts of Christ's death and its meaning:[8]

1) The cross has its effect entirely on humanity.

2) The cross has its effect primarily on hostile spiritual forces.

3) The cross has its effect first in God, who propitiated himself, and found full satisfaction in the atonement of Christ.

As Packer suggests, the third includes dimensions of the first and second. In other words, the atonement includes means by which persons actually do come to faith in Christ; it does have a necessary human dimension. Further, it also includes the fact that the atonement accomplished by Christ does indeed free us and does declare victory from hostile spiritual powers. But even as the penal substitutionary view of the atonement can include elements from the other groupings, the other groupings have primarily been originated in an effort to deny a penal substitutionary atonement, and even at times to avoid an objective understanding of the atonement.

In Mark Dever's recent *Christianity Today* article on the atonement,[9] he suggests that the three models of the atonement refer to three different sets of questions, or three different problems. The first is the assumption that humanity's great problem is that we are trapped and opposed by spiritual forces beyond our control. Is that true? Of course it's true. However, is that the central thrust of the atonement? No. Second, there are those who believe that the central problem is the subjective need of humanity to know God's love for us. Is that a legitimate need? Is that a true need? Is it accurate? Of course it is. Is that the central thrust of the atonement? Of course not. The third assumes that the main problem is God's righteous wrath against us for our sinfulness, which puts us under the verdict of eternal punishment.[10] Our need is for the full payment of the penalty for our sin—a penalty we cannot pay. This is the great central thrust of the biblical teaching on the atonement.

As we look at the penal substitutionary view of the atonement, I want to use a strategically chosen definition from the pen of I. Howard Marshall. This definition came in the midst of controversy within the Evangelical Alliance of Great Britain. Dr. Marshall argues that the penal substitutionary view of the atonement comprises two thoughts.[11]

First, humankind is condemned to eternal death as the penalty imposed by God upon human sin. No matter how much or how little we may have sinned, there is a fixed penalty for all sinners, namely, eternal death, of which physical death is both a part and a symbol. Hence arises the theological term *penal*, borrowed from legal categories.

Second, Dr. Marshall argues that the death of Christ on the cross was not merely a physical death but also the eternal death due to sinners. Christ did not suffer for his own sins, for he is without sin. Rather, Christ voluntarily bore the death due to other people because of their sins. His death was a substitute for the death of others. Consequently, those who accept Christ as savior are free from the penalty of their sins. He died in the place of sinners; hence the use of the theological term we have been using, *substitution*. True, sinners still die physically, unless they survive to the second coming and are transformed as a living people rather than raised from the dead. But they do not die eternally because Christ has died instead of them, and God will not require a penalty twice.

The reason why I chose Marshall's definition is not that I find it the most satisfactory or comprehensive. It is a very helpful defini-

tion, to be sure. The reason I chose that definition, quite strategically, is to indicate that the doctrine of substitution has been well
understood as a central part of the evangelical tradition. That is
to say, penal substitution is not a particular doctrine of Reformed
theologians, for Marshall is not part of the Reformed tradition.
Rather, penal substitution has been of importance to those who
would classify themselves as people of the cross. Furthermore, as
presented in Scripture, the atonement is both penal *and* substitutionary, a point Marshall makes clear. Efforts to divide the two, as
if it can be penal without being substitutionary or substitutionary
without being penal, make no sense.

Substitutionary Atonement and the Christian Tradition

The rejection of the penal or substitutionary understanding of
the atonement goes far back in terms of the history of the church.
Focusing specifically on the Reformation era, we find Fausto
Sozzini, better known as Socinus, who in the sixteenth century
opposed any understanding of the atonement that included any
operation whatsoever upon God. Socinus said that the atonement
must operate on humanity alone. Socinus becomes a model for our
understanding the larger problem of heresy. Denying a substitutionary understanding of the atonement, denying God's righteousness
and his justice, denying a penal requirement in terms of God's
response to sin, Socinus at least understood something of the full
impact of his teaching on the cross. These denials have serious
ramifications throughout the entire system of theology. Rarely is
that made clearer than in the case of Socinus, a heretic on more
than one count.

The debate on the substitutionary character of the atonement
certainly emerged in English-speaking theology in the nineteenth
and twentieth centuries. Horace Bushnell, for example, argued
against any objective understanding of the atonement in a way that
foresaw the coming of a classically liberal theology in the United

States. He argued that the atonement was a human-centered reality, part of a horizontal theology by which we are to learn the nature of true love from the self-sacrifice of Christ. James McCleod Campbell, Charles Finney, Vincent Taylor, and a series of others on both sides of the Atlantic engaged in intentional theological revisionism. They reformulated the doctrine of atonement to take away the scandal of substitution, desiring the removal of any "bloody cross religion."

In 1936, C. H. Dodd, a leading British New Testament scholar, wrote a book entitled *The Apostolic Preaching and Its Developments*.[12] Dodd offered what became a landmark argument against the substitutionary and penal understanding of Christ's work. He argued that the word *propitiation* had no place in the New Testament, even in terms of translation. Dodd's influence is felt in some translations of the Scripture, especially in *The New English Bible* which does not even include the word *propitiation*. In brief, Dodd worked to remove the scandal of any penal substitutionary understanding of the cross by redefining the work of Christ as merely expiation, not propitiation. In other words, Christ's atonement made amends for sin but did not effect any fundamental change in his disposition towards sinners.

In 1955 Leon Morris responded by publishing his Cambridge University doctrinal dissertation as a popular book entitled, *The Apostolic Preaching of the Cross*.[13] Morris, later warden at Tyndale House and principal at Ridley College in Melbourne, Australia, probably did more than any single evangelical in the midpoint of the twentieth century to reset the discussion on the atonement. He did so in two ways.

First, Morris worked directly against the errors of Dodd's work in terms of the language and grammar of the New Testament. Morris demonstrated that Dodd's work was incredibly dishonest, although he used typical British reserve. He would not have actually used that word, but if you read the footnotes, that is exactly what he is saying. He accused Dodd of borrowing some ideas and inventing others in order to argue that the Greek words simply *cannot* mean what they appear to mean. Second, Morris came back and argued that propitiation *presumes* and *includes* expiation, so that it is not an either/or alternative. The reality is that Christ not only became the penalty for our sin, but he also became the curse. He satisfied the divine justice by taking our sins away.

In 1973, Dr. Packer wrote his essay *What Did the Cross Achieve? The Logic of Penal Substitution*, presented as a Tyndale lecture at Cambridge University. It was presented in such a way that it was a theological alarm because, as Dr. Packer later reflected, he detected that among some who would call themselves evangelicals there was an uneasiness, a sense perhaps of theological and dogmatic and biblical insecurity, about the doctrine. Thus he wrote one of the clearest expositions—certainly found in the evangelical tradition—of the substitutionary atonement of Christ. From the 1970s on, it became clear that Dr. Packer's concern was well grounded.

Throughout the 1980s, revisionist evangelicals sought to revise the entire model and project of evangelical theology. In so doing, they desired to bring evangelical theology into a trajectory that would be free from so many of the scandals associated with truth claims that identified evangelicals in times past. And substitutionary atonement was one of those truth claims of greatest concern.

We fast-forward to 1994, when Clark Pinnock and Robert Brow wrote a book entitled, *Unbounded Love: A Good News Theology for the 21st Century*. Published by InterVarsity Press, this book clearly aimed to redefine the entire project of evangelical theology. Pinnock and Brow argued that the classic model of evangelical theology, including doctrines such as the inerrancy of Scripture and substitutionary atonement, was "a bad news theology." What was needed then was a "good news theology." The only way to turn a "bad news theology" into a "good news theology" was to work toward a "new reformation" in order to completely redefine the doctrine. They proposed, "We have to overcome the rational theory of the atonement, based in Latin judicial categories, that has dominated western theology."[14] They added, "We must realize that Jesus did not die in order to change God's attitude towards us, but to change our attitude towards God."[15]

The same publisher, InterVarsity Press, had published John Stott's book *The Cross of Christ* just eight years earlier, in 1986. In that book, Dr. Stott had written this: "We strongly reject, therefore, every explanation of the death of Christ which does not have as its centre the principle of 'satisfaction through substitution,' indeed divine self-satisfaction through divine self-substitution."[16]

Then, six years after publishing Pinnock and Brow, InterVarsity published *Recovering the Scandal of the Cross* by Joel Green and Mark Baker.[17] In the beginning chapters of the book, they state that their effort is to encourage evangelicals to supplement a penal substitutionary understanding of the atonement with other models. By the time you get to the center of the book, it is clear they do not want to *supplement* the doctrine of substitution, so much as to replace it. The language is unmistakable.

Two years later, in 2003, Steve Chalke and Alan Mann from Great Britain wrote *The Lost Message of Jesus*. Endorsed by figures such as N. T. Wright and Brian McClaren, the authors argued that the cross "isn't a form of cosmic child abuse," terminology they clearly associated with substitutionary atonement.[18] Some early reviewers of the book tried to indicate that in using this language, Chalke and Mann were not actually saying that the substitutionary understanding of the atonement presented a form of divine child abuse. However, in subsequent clarifications the authors made clear that this is indeed what they meant.

A controversy ensued within the Evangelical Alliance in Great Britain. Back in 1970 the Alliance had adopted a basis of faith which included this statement: "The substitutionary sacrifice of the incarnate Son of God as the sole all-sufficient ground of redemption from the guilt and power of sin, and from its eternal consequences."[19] This was then a necessary part of the group's confessional basis. Obviously, some of the authors of these books, Steve Chalke included, were calling into question the membership standards of the organization. All this led to an extensive controversy.

In July 2005 the "London Symposium on the Theology of the Atonement" was sponsored by the London School of Theology. At that historic symposium there was an open airing of all of these views. The Evangelical Alliance, that same year, modified its statement of faith to affirm the atonement in this way: "The atoning sacrifice of Christ on the cross, dying in our place, paying the price of sin and defeating evil, so reconciling us with God."[20] Notice what took place here. The controversy was occasioned, most pointedly, by those that claimed to be evangelical and had even signed the doctrinal basis of the Evangelical Alliance. But these members did not want to refer to the substitutionary death of Christ. No, as this debate made clear, some members of the Alliance openly opposed substitution and indeed published a work in which they characterized it explicitly as a form of divine child abuse. At the end of this process within the Evangelical Alliance, the group indicated that 90 percent of its members affirmed the substitutionary understanding of the atonement. Nevertheless, they changed the language in their confessional basis to *imply* substitution rather than to use the word explicitly.

Concerned about this, and determined to defend a penal substitutionary understanding of the atonement, Steve Jeffery, Mike Ovey, and Andrew Sach wrote a landmark book, *Pierced for Our Transgressions: Rediscovering the Glory of Penal Substitution.* They wrote, "The doctrine of penal substitution states that God gave himself in the person of his Son to suffer instead of us the death, punishment and curse due to fallen humanity as penalty for sin."[21] This understanding of the cross of Christ stands at the very heart of the gospel.

This strange but important chapter from the history of Britain's

Evangelical Alliance demonstrates the process of theological reductionism that so often accompanies confessional revisionism. In this case, a statement that clearly affirmed (and required) the substitutionary understanding of Christ's atonement was replaced with a statement that merely *implies* or *allows* for such an understanding. This becomes yet another illustration of the process Charles Spurgeon warned of in Britain's famous Downgrade Controversy of the nineteenth century.

When we fast-forward to the present hour, we understand that this controversy is not over, nor is it isolated to Great Britain or even to English-speaking theology. It is a controversy rampant across the Christian world. But most importantly, we notice that it is a controversy more concentrated among those who believe that the entire project of evangelical theology must be revised, especially among those who now claim that in a postmodern age we must form the gospel into something more fitting for postmodern categories and postmodern minds. In particular, we now see the substitutionary atonement being denied and subverted by many of those associated with the emerging church.[22]

Four Objections to Substitutionary Atonement

Drawing on the rich analysis found in *Pierced for Our Transgressions*, I want to organize the objections to substitutionary atonement around four large groups: (1) biblical, (2) theological, (3) moral, and (4) cultural. These are arbitrary in that there are few arguments that could be one of these without being another. However, some sort of typology is necessary for our present discussion.

Biblical Objections

Those who object on biblical grounds claim that we have misunderstood Scripture in whole or in part. They say we have the entire Bible story line wrong. In other words, going all the way back to the fall and arguing all the way forward to the cross and to God's acts

subsequent to the cross—from beginning to end—we supposedly
misconstrue the story line in seeing a message of penal substitutionary atonement.

First, some argue it is a misconstrual of *sin*. They say that sin
is not, first and foremost, an offense against God's righteousness
and holiness. Rather, it is entry into complicity with the powers of
darkness. It is a self-induced exile on the part of human creature.

Second, they argue that we misconstrue the *nature and character of God*. In particular, they say we misread biblical texts dealing
with divine wrath. Wherever Scripture references wrath, they say
it is merely a natural consequence of sin. Sin brings about its own
punishment. This redefinition of divine wrath is a recurrent theme.
They read a text such as Romans 1 and suggest that Paul was saying there that sin simply comes with its own punishment. Wrath is
being demonstrated or revealed as the necessary consequences of
sin. Now, does sin bring its own consequences? Of course! Just ask
someone who struggles with sin. Ask someone who has been victim-
ized by sin. Ask the apostle Paul. Sin, of course, does bring about its
own consequences, but those are not the consequences we should
most fear. The consequence to fear is the wrath of God poured out
upon all unrighteousness.

Third, they argue that *sacrifice* has been misunderstood. They
argue that the sacrificial animal was not being punished. The revi-
sionists argue that the sacrifice was merely a metaphor, a model that
was a symbol without anything objective taking place. Furthermore
they argue against understanding the Bible to say that God actually
required the sacrifice.

Fourth, they argue that we misconstrue *divine punishment*.
They say that the result of breaking God's law and covenant is
alienation first and foremost; we are separated from God. True, we
are in an alienated condition. However, in looking at the punish-
ments that follow sin, they suggest that this is merely the necessary
outpouring of consequences. They argue that divine punishment is

simply allowing the natural world and the natural order God has put into place to work out its own consequences. The removal of God's personal offendedness and his personal wrath poured upon sin greatly misconstrues the message of the Bible.

Look at just one particular text, Isaiah 53, where we find the image of the suffering servant. Critics of substitutionary atonement argue that the language here should be properly understood not as suffering *for us*, or *on our behalf as a substitute*, but rather as an identification *with us*, a suffering *alongside us*. Given their understanding, one would answer Anselm's question, "Why the Incarnation?" (*Cur Deus Homo?*), by asserting, "God became man in order to identify with us and to suffer along with us, even to the point of the cross, in order to enter into the deepest brokenness of our humanity."

Fifth, it follows then that they argue that we misconstrue prophetic expectation, such as in the previous passage from Isaiah. In other words, Isaiah must not have been looking for one who would redeem people from sin. Rather, in historical context, Isaiah sought for one who would free and liberate.

Sixth, they argue that we misconstrue the use of the Old Testament in the New Testament. They suggest we are simply reading back onto the Old Testament categories that we wish to find in the New Testament. But when we turn to the New Testament, they say we reverse course and read it in fulfillment of the Old Testament texts that we have already interpreted in light of the New Testament expectations that we have imported to the text. Here we confront a truly important question: who gets to interpret the Old Testament? I must argue strongly that the inspired New Testament authors have this privilege, first of all. At this point the issue of biblical authority inevitably arises. It is patently inconsistent to claim a high view of biblical authority and then to assert that the New Testament authors misunderstand the Old Testament.

Seventh, they suggest that we misread the words of Jesus in

terms of his self-understanding. Amazingly, Joel Green and Mark Baker argue that in the New Testament we have no direct access to Jesus' self-understanding of the cross and of his death, because, "He never wrote anything." That is a reminder to us that a denial of penal substitution is never "naked," to use Luther's expression about doctrine. It is always connected to other doctrines. They argue that we misconstrue the language of the New Testament concerning the wrath of God and God's disposition toward sinners.

Finally, to quickly review some other lines of attack, critics of penal substitutionary atonement argue that we misconstrue the necessity of a sacrifice for sin as payment. They suggest that we misconstrue the victory achieved by Christ. They suggest that we minimize the resurrection when we focus upon the cross. And they suggest that we miss the fact that the central message of Jesus is non-violence.

Interestingly enough, there are some who reject a penal substitutionary view of the atonement with full and bracing honesty, admitting that the Bible does teach it but rejecting it anyway. They argue that it is simply unacceptable in the twenty-first century to believe this. In terms of intellectual integrity, I have far more intellectual respect for someone who admits rejecting what the Bible teaches than for someone who attempts to deny that the Bible teaches what it clearly *does* teach.

Theological Objections

In terms of theological objections, the central concern has to do with the rendering of God made necessary by a penal substitutionary view of the atonement. This is centered on the fact that God's holiness and righteousness and justice define his love, even as his love defines his righteousness and his justice and his wrath. The entire concept of God's wrath is completely unthinkable to some theologians and figures in the twenty-first century, even as we might argue that it has been considered unacceptable by figures throughout the history of the church. The whole idea of retributive justice and punishment for sin is now commonly rejected. Socinus rejected it; now Steve Chalke rejects it in the sense that he proposes that God orders us to be peaceful and to resist violence.[23] Therefore, he argues that any suggestion that God requires violence as a punishment for sin makes God hypocritical. Chalke argues that any understanding of retributive justice presents a form of divine revenge.

One of the figures behind all this is Walter Wink. In his book *Engaging the Powers*, Wink suggests that the sole message of the cross is the victory of non-violence over violence.[24] Therefore, he asserts that the entire understanding of the atonement has to be redefined so as to take away any necessity of the death of Christ. Instead, Christ must be presented as the *victim* who overcomes by his innocence rather than as a second person of the Trinity, the sinless Son of God, who became incarnate in order to humble himself, taking on the form of a man and dying as a substitution for sinners.

In *Unbounded Love* Clark Pinnock and Robert Brow present a breathtaking proposal:

> We have to overcome the rational theory of atonement based on Latin judicial categories, that has dominated Western theology. It demotes the resurrection from its central place and changes the cross from scandal to abstract theory. It makes things sound as if God *wanted* Jesus to die and predestined Pilate and Caiaphus to make it happen. Surely not—Jesus is God's beloved Son. The Father and the Son are not divided or in opposition.[25]

There is a great deal of biblical truth here. Jesus *is* God's beloved Son. There *is* no division or opposition between the Father and the Son. But these truths are distorted when it is suggested that this means that the Father did not will the death of the Son. Pinnock and Brow explicitly deny that God predestined the cross—a direct refutation of the apostolic preaching in Acts 2. But they do not stop at this point. They also assert a completely subjective understanding of the atonement:

> The cross demonstrates the compassion of God. Through the surrender of Jesus, God seeks out lost sinners, enters into their forsakenness and brings them into an unbreakable fellowship. Let us try to set our thinking about atonement in personal, not legalistic terms. The real issue is a broken relationship, not a breach of contract. Before the cross happened, God loved sinners and wanted to save them. The cross did not purchase love for sinners. It is we, not God, who need to be changed in attitude. The problem of salvation is our need to be delivered from the power of evil and become people who love God again.[26]

They go on to explain:

> Christ is not appeasing God's wrath. God is not sadistically crucifying His beloved Son. We are not talking about retribution or criminal proceedings. The cross is a revelation of a compassionate God. Suffering love is the way of salvation for sinners. Jesus takes the pain or divine love on himself in solidarity with all of us. This tells us that God remains faithful to his creatures, even though they have abandoned him; he desires that they live and not die. This is how God justifies us and brings us back to life.[27]

Finally:

> We must realize that Jesus did not die in order to change God's attitude towards us, but to change our attitude towards God. God, who took the initiative of reconciling the world, does not need reconciling. It is in us that the decisive change is needed.[28]

Pinnock and Brow go on in *Unbounded Love* to acknowledge that the cross has an objective side as well. They even accept that it is possible to speak of propitiation in "non-legal" terms (by which they mean non-substitutionary terms). What kind of impact would

the cross then have on God—the propitiation of his wrath? No! It
is, for God, an educational experience. They argue that, in experiencing suffering through the incarnation—Jesus Christ as the divine
human being—God learned how to identify with us, and thus some
moral change is wrought in God.

In *Recovering the Scandal of the Cross* Joel Green and Mark
Baker get to the heart of their opposition to penal substitutionary
atonement when they write:

> Understanding sin narrowly as an infraction of the laws of God
> falls short of the biblical account of sin. This is perhaps trouble-
> some enough, but linking this view of sin with a Western penal
> view of justice also proposes, and for some even requires, a con-
> cept of God that is incongruent with the biblical witness.[29]

With these words, Green and Baker insinuate that "the biblical
writers" present a God who loves without requiring an atonement for sin. Yet in order to maintain this conclusion one is forced
to deny clear teachings of the Bible that *do* make clear that God
requires a penalty for sin and does so as a function of his holiness
and character. They continue:

> Unfortunately, trying to nuance the meaning of this model in the
> pages of a theology book has not proven sufficient to protect
> people in the pew from the damaging effects of the image of God
> this model communicates and seems to demand. Tragically, many
> Christians (and former believers) still live in fear of a God who
> seems so intent on punishing, and much less willing to forgive,
> than folks we encounter in day-to-day life.[30]

Here we face what is missing (or denied?) in their analysis. There
is a fundamental difference between human forgiveness and divine
forgiveness, and this is central to understanding Scripture. *We* can
forgive wrongs done to us, but we cannot atone for them. And first
and foremost, these acts are not offenses against *our* righteousness,

for we have none. To model atonement on human forgiveness and to suggest that God is less forgiving than our neighbors is a slander against Christ and his work—and against the character of God.

Moral Objections

In terms of the moral objections to the cross, we come back to the accusations of such things as "divine child-abuse." Donald Capps of Princeton Theological Seminary has attempted to demonstrate that the problem of child abuse in this society is deeply rooted in a substitutionary understanding of the cross. He argues that such concepts lead to the belief that children are supposed to suffer in redemptive suffering.[31]

Many of these moral objections follow the French philosopher and literary scholar René Girard, who suggests in three books—*The Scapegoat*; *Things Hidden Since the Foundation of the World*; and *Violence and the Sacred*—that human conflict comes down to what he calls "victimage."[32] He suggests that crude primitive religion included sacrifice through what he calls "the scapegoat mechanism." He then suggests that the New Testament subverts what the Old Testament asserts and that the New Testament repudiates the entire sacrificial system. He argues that what Jesus accomplished was dying as a scapegoat in order to end the scapegoat mechanism. As the truly innocent one, Jesus died as the innocent scapegoat, recognized to be innocent in order to bring an end to the "scapegoat project."

You look at that and rightly think, "That sounds so foreign. What in the world could that have to do with contemporary evangelical theology?" But trace the footnotes of theologians and authors who are revising the atonement. See how often Girard, his works, and "the scapegoat mechanism" appear, especially among the emerging church types who want to reject the penal substitutionary understanding of the atonement. Get this clear: Girard asserts that the Old Testament is *wrong*, and that the sacrificial system was a crude anthropological borrowing from primitive society. He argues that even in the Old Testament you can see people grow in moral revulsion against the sacrificial system, so that when you have the prophets making very clear statements that God doesn't demand sacrifice, you can see how they're distancing themselves. Steve Chalke, in the debate in London in 2005, used the same argument, stating that the prophets began to understand the error of the sacrificial system as well. Just consider what that says about the authority and inerrancy of Scripture.

In another example of moral objections, well-known feminist theologian Susan Brooks-Thistlethwaite offered her complaint against the substitutionary atonement in *Time* magazine:

> Countless women have told me that their priest or minister had advised them, as "good Christian women" to accept beatings by their husbands as "Christ accepted the cross." An overemphasis on the suffering of Jesus to the exclusion of his teaching has tended to be used to support violence.[33]

I don't know what you do with this, but I want to ask a journalistic question: where are these countless women, so that we can find their pastors? Let me state pointedly that I do not believe this. In decades of evangelical experience I have never even heard these ideas mentioned. Evangelicals must address the horrible violence experienced by so many women at the hands of sinful men, but this does not lead to a denial of the atonement whereby the innocent Son of God died in the place of sinners.

Cultural Objections

Cultural objections come in the form of complaints about the irrelevance of the doctrine. Pinnock and Brow suggest that a new theology has to be *compelling* because the old theology held by evangelicals does not present a compelling sense of truth anymore to postmodern people. They propose that if we are going to be relevant to a postmodern world, we have to come up with something compelling. The word *relevant* is exactly what Green and Baker are using in suggesting that the whole idea of penal substitution doesn't apply to people who don't think they're sinners in the first place. In other words, we will not be taken seriously if we tell people that they are personally in need of a savior.

Why do they hate it so? Well, the Bible becomes an embarrassment to those who reject the idea that God required a violent penalty for sin. This notion of God requiring punishment for sin is completely unacceptable to postmodern people, we are told. Some of those who reject a penal substitutionary atonement also reject the fact that God would order the execution or killing of *anyone* for *any* reason. Some go so far as to reject the claim that God would require a sacrifice of an animal in the Old Testament, much less the self-sacrifice of himself through Christ in his substitutionary atonement.

God's wrath is eagerly rejected. God's holiness is redefined to eliminate the need for sin. The imputation of Adam's sin to us and the necessity (through the substitutionary atonement) of the grace of God demonstrated in the imputation of Christ's righteousness to the elect is rejected. Some then want to redesign salvation so that it has more to do with enlightenment, moral improvement, a surrendering of claims to power and a breaking of the "empire system" in terms of political power, and the establishment of the kingdom of God over against earthly kingdoms.

One dimension of this controversy often overlooked is the link between substitutionary atonement and the exclusivity of the gospel of Christ. Put simply, if the atonement is entirely subjective in its design and effects, any number of alternative ways to subjective change might suffice. If nothing *objective* happened in the atonement of Christ, the claim that Jesus is the only savior loses an essential biblical connection.

Finally, justification by faith alone is undercut by a denial of a penal substitutionary understanding of the atonement. It undercuts the church, the redeemed people of God. And it undercuts eschatology because there is no hell (or at least no hell in terms of the just punishment of unrepentant sinners under the wrath of God). Sally Brown, in her book *Cross Talk*, asserts that the problem for those, like herself, who reject the substitutionary atonement is that it keeps rearing its head over and over again, because when you get Christians together they'll find a way to sing it.[34] So true. Just ask Charles Wesley.

Pastoral Implications

Finally, I offer some pastoral implications. First, substitution is central to our understanding of the cross. Second, there is always more to the cross than any one conceptual framework can bear, but it is nevertheless the truth that the central biblical message is that of substitution. Third, there is no way to modify the gospel without repudiating the gospel. We can modify our *presentation* of the gospel, but we must be very careful not to modify the gospel itself. Fourth, there is no way to present the gospel without speaking directly of our sin and of God's gracious provision through Christ—the full satisfaction of God's justice. Fifth, a therapeutic age demands a therapeutic gospel, which means that we really are the problem. We do not want to admit this and will gladly grab and clasp any straw that argues that we are victims rather than perpetrators of the great crime. Sixth, penal substitution is the only adequate biblical explanation for how God remains both just and merciful. As Romans 3 makes clear, God is both just and Justifier. Seventh, we must consider carefully legitimate criticisms of any expression of doctrine. In this light, I want to argue that at times we have argued for an overly individualistic understanding of the atonement. We must remember that God's purpose is to bring glory to his name through the creation of a people purchased by his Son. Eighth, sinners desperately need to hear the great truth of the gospel and to be safe from the wrath to come. God's redeemed people must exult and rest in the sure confidence that God will indeed bring all things to completion.

Charles Wesley had it right, and we rightly sing those words that exult in the truth that Jesus Christ died in the place of sinners in order that we might know full pardon and salvation. The denial of the substitutionary character of Christ's atonement is no small matter. Indeed, it represents a direct assault against the integrity of the gospel of Jesus Christ. Those who stand together for the gospel must also stand against any effort to rob that gospel of its truth and power.

CHAPTER 7

HOW DOES THE SUPREMACY OF CHRIST CREATE RADICAL CHRISTIAN SACRIFICE?

A Meditation on the Book of Hebrews

John Piper

I invite you to look with me at a sequence of six passages in the New Testament book of Hebrews. These six passages contain the answer to the question contained in the title of this message, "How Does the Supremacy of Christ Create Radical Christian Sacrifice?" But for you to see it, you will need to ask, what is the great reward, and what is the better resurrection, and what is the joy set before us, and what is the city that is to come? My answer to all these questions is the same: their most ultimate meaning is that they refer to the infinite supremacy of Christ experienced with all-satisfying joy. The sequence is as follows.

Hebrews 10:32-35:

> But recall the former days when, after you were enlightened, you endured a hard struggle with sufferings, sometimes being publicly exposed to reproach and affliction, and sometimes being partners with those so treated. For you had compassion on those in prison, and you joyfully accepted the plundering of your property, since

you knew that you yourselves had a better possession and an abiding one. Therefore do not throw away your confidence, which has a great reward.[1]

Hebrews 11:6:

And without faith it is impossible to please him, for whoever would draw near to God must believe that he exists and that he rewards those who seek him.

Hebrews 11:24–26:

By faith Moses, when he was grown up, refused to be called the son of Pharaoh's daughter, choosing rather to be mistreated with the people of God than to enjoy the fleeting pleasures of sin. He considered the reproach of Christ greater wealth than the treasures of Egypt, for he was looking to the reward.

Hebrews 11:35:

Some were tortured, refusing to accept release, so that they might rise again to a better life.

Hebrews 12:2:

Looking to Jesus, the founder and perfecter of our faith, who for the joy that was set before him endured the cross, despising the shame, and is seated at the right hand of the throne of God.

Hebrews 13:12–14:

So Jesus also suffered outside the gate in order to sanctify the people through his own blood. Therefore let us go to him outside the camp and bear the reproach he endured. For here we have no lasting city, but we seek the city that is to come.

We will come back to this sequence later. But let me put these texts and the question I am posing in a wider context of my hopes for you and for this message.

Radically Flavored Life and Ministry

My desire and prayer for you is that your life and ministry have a radical flavor, a risk-taking flavor: a gutsy, countercultural, wartime flavor that makes the average prosperous Americans in your church feel uncomfortable; a strange mixture of tenderness and toughness that keeps worldly people a little off balance; a pervasive summons to something more and something hazardous and something wonderful; a saltiness and brightness, something like the life of Jesus.

When Jesus said, "You are the salt of the earth" and "You are the light of the world" (Matt. 5:13–14), I think he was referring to the preceding verses where he had described the most outrageous joy imaginable: "Blessed are you when others revile you and persecute you and utter all kinds of evil against you falsely on my account. Rejoice and be glad, for your reward is great in heaven" (Matt. 5:11–12). Be glad when you are persecuted and slandered.

Bright and Salty in Trials

My desire for you is that your life and ministry taste like that. Reviling comes. Persecution comes. Slander comes. And you rejoice that you are counted worthy to be shamed for the name of Jesus (see Acts 5:41). And you preach and live in such a way that over a decade or two or three, those in your church come to be bright and salty like that—counting it all joy when they meet various trials, because you have taught them and shown them that they have a great reward in heaven—the all-satisfying, everlasting experience of the supremacy of Christ.

You have lived. You have treasured Christ above the accumulation of stuff. You have laid up treasures in heaven, not on earth. You have fled not only fornication and adultery but also opulence and ostentation and riches. You have remembered the story of the rich young man (Luke 18:18–30). And you have blazoned on the walls of your mind the words of Paul: "Those who desire to be rich fall into temptation, into a snare, into many senseless and harmful desires that plunge people into ruin and destruction" (1 Tim. 6:9–10). You have eaten the words of Isaiah, and they have become sweet to your soul: "All flesh is like grass and all its glory like the flower of grass. The grass withers, and the flower falls, but the word of the Lord remains forever" (1 Pet. 1:24–25).

Awakening a Sense of Christ's Value

My desire and prayer for you is that your life and ministry have a radical flavor. I say that for the glory of Christ. The world does not glorify Jesus as their supreme Treasure because of our health, wealth, and prosperity. Those are the same treasures they live for. The fact that we use Jesus to get what they want makes it clear to them that we have the same treasure as they do—and it is not Jesus. He's just the ticket. And tickets are thrown away when the show begins.

What the world is waiting to see—what might awaken a sense of Christ's value—is something radical. Some risk. Some crazy sacrifice. Some extraordinary love. Something salty and bright. They may not like it when they see it. They may crucify it. But they will not be bored. Stephen's face shown like an angel (Acts 6:15). His wisdom was irresistible (Acts 6:10). So they killed him. But they did not yawn, and they did not go to sleep. And Acts 8 makes clear his death was not in vain.

Where Are God's Men?

My desire and prayer for you is that your life and ministry have a radical flavor—the flavor of risk, sacrifice, love, simplicity, joy, freedom, and precarious adventure. In 1939, Howard Guinness, one of the early founders of the International Fellowship of Evangelical Students, wrote a little book called *Sacrifice*. He was trying to do then what I am trying to do now. He wrote:

Where are the young men and women of this generation who will hold their lives cheap, and be faithful even unto death, who will lose their lives for Christ's, flinging them away for love of him? Where are those who will live dangerously, and be reckless in this service? Where are the men of prayer? Where are the men who count God's Word of more importance to them than their daily food? Where are the men who, like Moses of old, commune with God face to face as a man speaks with his friend? Where are God's men in this day of God's power?[2]

Indeed, where are the pastors who say with the apostle Paul, "I do not account my life of any value nor as precious to myself, if only I may finish my course and the ministry that I received from the Lord Jesus, to testify to the gospel of the grace of God" (Acts 20:24)?

Where are the pastors who say with Joab to his brother Abishai, when surrounded by Syrians and Ammonites, "Be of good courage, and let us be courageous for our people, and for the cities of our God, and may the Lord do what seems good to him" (2 Sam. 10:12)?

Where are the young women—single and married—who say with Esther, when the life of her people hung in the balance and Mordecai asked her to risk her life, "I will go to the king, though it is against the law, and if I perish, I perish" (Est. 4:16)?

The Certainty of Suffering

I ask you this not just because the world desperately needs to see that kind of pastor, but also because Jesus makes it crystal clear that if you take him seriously, you are going to suffer. In other words, radical willingness to risk and sacrifice and suffer is the only authentic ministry there is. The Lord has made it very plain:

If anyone would come after me, let him deny himself and take up his cross and follow me. (Matt. 16:24)

If they have called the master of the house Beelzebul, how much more will they malign those of his household. (Matt. 10:25)

"A servant is not greater than his master." If they persecuted me, they will also persecute you. (John 15:20)

They will lay their hands on you and persecute you, delivering you up to the synagogues and prisons, and you will be brought before kings and governors for my name's sake. . . . You will be delivered up even by parents and brothers and relatives and friends, and some of you they will put to death. You will be hated by all for my name's sake. But not a hair of your head will perish. By your endurance you will gain your lives. (Luke 21:12–19)

The hour is coming when whoever kills you will think he is offering service to God. (John 16:2)

God Promises Trials

And after Jesus, Paul made this teaching the bedrock of his counsel to new believers. On his way back from the first missionary journey, he was teaching the new disciples in every church "through many tribulations we must enter the kingdom of God" (Acts 14:22). He adds in 2 Timothy 3:12, "All who desire to live a godly life in Christ Jesus will be persecuted."

Then he poses the question in Romans 8:35, "Who shall separate us from the love of Christ? Shall tribulation, or distress, or persecution, or famine, or nakedness, or danger, or sword?" Of course, the answer is no. But is the answer no because God spares us these things or because he ordains these things for us and keeps us in them? The next verse gives the answer: "As it is written, 'For your sake we are being killed all the day long; we are regarded as sheep to be slaughtered.' No, in all these things we are more than conquerors through him who loved us" (Rom. 8:36–37). God does not spare his people these trials. He promises them.

"Why Not Me?"

So does Hebrews 12:8: "If you are left without discipline . . . then you are illegitimate children and not sons." Suffering for followers of Christ is a sign of God's merciful fatherhood. And it includes all the pains of the world in general. That's what Romans 8:23 makes plain: "Not only the creation, but we ourselves, who have the first-fruits of the Spirit, groan inwardly as we wait eagerly for adoption as sons, the redemption of our bodies."

> Sir Norman Anderson, former Professor and Director of the Advanced Legal Institute at London University, supported International Fellowship of Evangelical Students for sixty years. He had lost all three of his children in their early adulthood and his wife was so senile she could not recognize him. At one of the last public events where he spoke he was asked, "When you look back over your life and reflect on the fact that you have lost all your three children, and how your wife of sixty years no longer recognizes you, do you ever ask the question, 'Why me?' . . . "No, I've never asked that question, 'Why me?' but I have asked the question, 'Why not me?' I am not promised as a Christian that I will escape the problems encountered by others; we all live in a fallen world. . . . I am however, promised that in the midst of difficulties, God through Christ will be present with me, and will give his grace to help me cope with the difficulties and bear witness to him."[3]

"Beloved, do not be surprised at the fiery trial when it comes upon you to test you, as though something strange were happening to you" (1 Pet. 4:12–13). Jesus, Paul, Peter, the book of Hebrews—they all bear witness: followers of Jesus will suffer. I do not want to be excluded from that number.

> *Must I be carried to the skies*
> *On flowery beds of ease,*
> *While others fought to win the prize,*
> *And sailed through bloody seas?*

My desire and prayer for you is that you will not even try to be carried to the skies on flowery beds of ease, but that there will be a radical, risk-taking, sacrificial flavor to your life and ministry.

What Creates Radical Christian Sacrifice?

My questions are: What creates such a life and ministry? What creates radical Christian sacrifice? And how is it created? There is more than one biblical answer to these questions. So please don't take this as exhaustive.

To answer, let's turn back to the book of Hebrews, where we began. What I hope you will see is that the aim of the book of Hebrews is precisely the same as my aim in this essay—a life and ministry of radical risk and sacrificial love, all for the glory of Christ. The way the writer creates that radical risk and sacrifice is by giving some of the most elaborate and magnificent glimpses of the supremacy of Christ in all the Bible.

Hebrews: A Word of Exhortation

We know that Hebrews is one of the most doctrinally sophisticated books in the Bible. What we don't realize as often is that it is probably the only instance in the New Testament of a sermon delivered to Christians[4]—as opposed to the sermons in Acts directed mainly to unbelievers. This sermon (he calls it a "word of exhortation," Heb. 13:22) was delivered in the hope of creating in the Christian hearers a commitment to radical, joyful, risk-taking sacrifices of love that make Christ look as great as he really is. The vision of Christ's supremacy that runs through the book is there to serve this radical, practical, public aim. So consider the sequence of texts we looked at earlier, only notice very carefully now how radical, joyful, risk-taking, sacrificial love is created.

Joyfully Accepting Plundered Possessions

> But recall the former days when, after you were enlightened, you endured a hard struggle with sufferings, sometimes being publicly exposed to reproach and affliction, and sometimes being partners with those so treated. For you had compassion on those in prison, and you joyfully accepted the plundering of your property, since

you knew that you yourselves had a better possession and an abiding one. Therefore do not throw away your confidence, which has
a great reward. (Heb. 10:32–35)

Some believers had been imprisoned. Others had suffered by
standing with them. What created the radical, sacrificial love of
standing with the prisoners and paying the price of having their
property plundered? The answer is in the middle of verse 34: "You
joyfully accepted the plundering of your property, *since you knew*
[*ginōskontes*] that you yourselves had a better possession and an
abiding one." Verse 35 calls this "better possession and abiding
one" a "great reward."

What created this radical, sacrificial act of love toward imprisoned saints was the superior Treasure they were banking on in the
future. This confidence of heavenly reward made them joyful in
earthly loss. They *joyfully* accepted the plundering of their property.
That is what I am saying is needed in your life and ministry—and
then in your people. Hold your possessions so loosely that when
they are lost in the sacrifices of love, your confidence in a supreme
Treasure in heaven will fill you with joy. I am going to argue in a
moment that the Treasure is the supremacy of Christ. [5]

Looking to the Reward

By faith Moses, when he was grown up, refused to be called the
son of Pharaoh's daughter, choosing rather to be mistreated with
the people of God than to enjoy the fleeting pleasures of sin. He
considered the reproach of Christ greater wealth than the treasures of Egypt, for he was looking to the reward. (Heb. 11:24–26)

How was Moses' radical, loving sacrifice created? "He considered
the reproach of Christ greater wealth than the treasures of Egypt,
for he was looking to the reward." Present sacrifice is sustained
by the hope of future reward. Again I will argue that the reward is
finally Christ himself in all his glory.

Enduring the Cross for the Joy Set before Him

> Looking to Jesus, the founder and perfecter of our faith, who
> for the joy that was set before him endured the cross, despising
> the shame, and is seated at the right hand of the throne of God.
> (Heb. 12:2)

How was Jesus' radical, loving sacrifice sustained? It was sustained
by "the joy that was set before him." That's how he endured the
cross. He looked forward to the triumphant experience of being
exalted as the Savior and Lord and Treasure of an innumerable
people beyond the grave and beyond this age. Even as he suffers *for*
us, he shows us how to suffer *with* him. He models the very motive
that we see in the other texts of this sequence. Indestructible joy
breaking into present suffering from the assurance of future joy.

Seeking the City That Is to Come

> Jesus also suffered outside the gate in order to sanctify the people
> through his own blood. Therefore let us go to him outside the
> camp and bear the reproach he endured. For here we have no
> lasting city, but we seek the city that is to come. (Heb. 13:12–14)

In the end comes the summons that I have been issuing all along—
the radical call. This is why I said the book of Hebrews is aiming
at the very thing I am aiming at in this message—that your life and
ministry will have a radical, risk-taking, sacrificial flavor. Hebrews
bids us do something like that, something outlandish: "Let us go
to him outside the camp and bear the reproach he endured." What
does that mean for you? It means something radical. Something
risk-taking. Something sacrificial. God will make it plain if you will
say to him, "Anything, Lord. Anytime. Anywhere." If your heart is
yielded, he will make it plain.

But again I ask: how is this radical, risk-taking, sacrificial life
created and sustained? The answer is in verse 14, and it is the same
answer we have seen in chapters 10, 11, and 12: "For here we have

no lasting city, but we seek the city that is to come." Radical, risk-taking, sacrificial acts of love "outside the camp" are created and sustained by treasuring the final city of God more than the present city of man, no matter how rich this present city seems.

What Is the Reward?

So at least part of the structure of how radical sacrifice is created is clear: it is created when we treasure our future reward vastly more than we treasure the comforts and securities of ordinary earthly life. Really believing, really treasuring, really cherishing and valuing—*what* in the future? What treasure, what reward, is the key to creating and sustaining a life and ministry of radical, risk-taking, sacrificial love?

My answer is that all of the book of Hebrews is about the supremacy of Jesus Christ as the Treasure to be trusted in, hoped for, banked on, cherished, and valued beyond everything this present life can offer.

Really? Isn't Jesus Christ presented in the book of Hebrews as the *means* to our salvation? Is he the end? Is he the Reward? Or is he the means to obtaining the reward? Isn't he presented as making purification for sins (1:3; 2:9; 2:17; 9:24; 10:12) and interceding as our High Priest (2:17; 4:14; 7:17) and becoming the "founder of salvation" (2:10) and the perfecter of our faith (12:2)? Yes.

The Glory of Jesus' Person Displayed in His Saving Work

But here is what I have been learning in the last several years as never before. The supreme greatness and majesty and glory of the Son of God fit him to be the saving means of our justification and forgiveness and propitiation and sanctification and eternal life. But in that very means-work on the cross, the apex of his glory in them is displayed in the freedom of grace. And in the very moment of becoming the perfect means of our redemption, Christ becomes the supremely valuable, all-glorious end of our redemption (John 17:24). The glory that we will see and savor forever and ever will be the glory of the Lamb who was slain (Rev. 5:9, 12–13). That is the song of eternity. The final beauty that will satisfy our souls forever is the beauty most fully displayed in the rescue of sinners to see that beauty.

Therefore, I say that all the pictures of the supremacy of Jesus in the book of Hebrews are pictures not only of the perfection of the all-sufficient *means* of our salvation but also of the all-satisfying goal or end of our salvation, namely, the supremacy of Christ himself experienced with all-satisfying joy. He is the Great Reward. He is the one we know in the "better life." He is the light of the city that is to come.

Therefore everything this epistle says about him intensifies our love for him now as our treasure, and our desire for him later as our final reward. He is:

- God's final revelation (1:2);
- The heir of all things (1:2);
- The creator of the world (1:2);
- The radiance of God's glory (1:3);
- The exact imprint of God's nature (1:3).

Also:

- He upholds the universe by the word of his power (1:3).
- He made purification for sins (1:3).
- He sits at the right hand of the Majesty on High (1:4).
- He is God, enthroned forever, with a scepter of uprightness (1:8).
- His rule will have no end (1:8).
- He is worshiped by angels (1:6).
- His joy is above all other beings in the universe (1:9).
- He was crowned with glory and honor because of his suffering (2:9).

- He was the founder of our salvation (2:10).
- He was made perfect in all his obedience by his suffering (2:10).
- He took on human flesh (2:14).
- He destroyed the one who has the power of death, the Devil (2:14).
- He delivered us from the bondage of fear (2:15).
- He is a merciful and faithful high priest (2:17).
- He made propitiation for sins (2:17).
- He is sympathetic because of his own trials (4:15).
- He never sinned (4:15).
- He offered up loud cries and tears with reverent fear, and God heard him (5:7).
- He became the source of eternal salvation (5:8).
- He holds his priesthood by virtue of an indestructible life (7:16).
- He appears in the presence of God on our behalf (9:24).
- He will come a second time to save us who are eagerly waiting for him (9:28).
- He is the same yesterday, today, and forever (13:8).

All of this supremacy of Christ is poured into the word "him" in Hebrews 13:13: "Therefore let us go *to him* outside the camp and bear the reproach he endured." To him!

Come to Me—Outside the Camp

When he bids us leave the securities and comforts of life and take up a radical, risk-taking, sacrificial way of love in his service, it is not a path that we take alone. In fact, Jesus is there outside the camp in a way that he is nowhere else. He is not just telling us to go out there. He is inviting us come out here. Here is where I am. Come to *me* outside the camp.

The supremacy of Christ is not just his perfect fitness to bear our sins, and not just the supremely valuable future reward that frees us from fear and greed and worldliness, but in his supremacy he is also now our present, personal Treasure.

And there he is outside the camp bidding us come. The sweetest fellowship with Jesus you will ever know is the fellowship of his sufferings.

So I say it one more time: my desire and prayer to God for you is that your life and ministry have a radical, risk-taking, sacrificial flavor.

Let us go to him outside the camp. For here we have no lasting city. But we seek a city which is to come, whose builder is God and whose light is the Lamb.

CHAPTER 8

SUSTAINING THE PASTOR'S SOUL

C. J. Mahaney

I'm not sure how to describe an event like Together for the Gospel. When asked about the conference, I've simply said it was extraordinary and unforgettable. During those three days in Louisville, we listened to world-class preaching from world-class pastors. We were equipped to love the Savior more passionately and serve our churches more effectively. We experienced the nearness of God in worship, joining with 5,500 other voices in singing praise to the Savior. Our conversations, whether serious or humorous, prolonged our mealtimes and lasted late into the night. Every time we walked into the auditorium, we found new stacks of free books on our seats (and what makes a pastor happier than free books?). We had only to walk across the hall to browse a massive, well-stocked bookstore, where we added armfuls of books to our piles of free ones. We ate well and drank coffee like we had no Starbucks budget.

But as the conference drew to a close, we began to contemplate the challenges that waited for us at home. I'm sure you have experienced that transition from conference life to normal life. As the conference ends, you begin to think about the demands of preparing another sermon. You feel the weight of the unanswered e-mails that have accumulated in your absence. You think about people in your church in need of care and correction and comfort. You are keenly aware that a day at the Together for the Gospel conference bears little resemblance to your normal day as a pastor.

In an article in *Tabletalk* magazine, Peter Alwinson describes the life of a pastor, painting a personal and candid picture of the difference between naïve expectations and (sometimes harsh) reality:

> It was going to be relatively simple, this work of pastoring: Jesus had come, He had endured . . . and conquered with blinding glory the cross and tomb. In His own words, "In the world you will have tribulation; but be of good cheer, I have overcome the world" (John 16:33b) and, "Say to them, 'The kingdom of God has come near to you'" (Luke 10:9b).
>
> Teach and preach the Word with accuracy, clarity, and practicality and they will come and they will mature and together we will win the world for King Jesus, with King Jesus at our side. Not an uncommon perspective for a seminarian with divinity degree freshly in hand. It was my earnest conviction and expectation. . . .
>
> Cracks quickly appeared in that sanguine theological position. Idealism and incomplete theology must after all eventually give way to reality. Worship attendance grows; babies die and have to be buried; a businessman becomes hungry for God and receives Christ; a convert slips back to the drug lifestyle and is on the streets again; marriage partners are reconciled; Christians bicker with their brothers in Christ. . . .
>
> The "already-not-yetness" of the kingdom of God is in the practical theology department for pastors. We live it and witness it every day. . . . Blessing, power, and joy alternate daily and rapidly with loss, weakness, and grief. Church life is a carousel of defeat and victory.[1]

Perhaps you recognize yourself somewhere in this description. If you have been in ministry for more than a few days, you are familiar with this carousel.

In this final chapter, I want to have a personal word with you. I want to prepare you for the challenges that await you on the "carousel of defeat and victory" where "blessing, power, and joy alternate daily and rapidly with loss, weakness, and grief." I want to address your heart and care for your soul.

Every chapter in the book so far has been designed to equip you with gospel-centered, doctrinal discernment. As pastors, we need to be armed to contend for the truth of the gospel and, where necessary, to humbly and courageously oppose error and protect the churches that we love and serve. We need to be reminded that there is no true pastoral ministry apart from faithful gospel proclamation and doctrinal precision.

But pastoral ministry demands not only faithful proclamation of the gospel, but also personal holiness. It demands not only doctrinal precision, but also godly affection; not only public proclamation, but also pleasing God in the privacy of our hearts. Pastoral ministry is not only about our minds, but also about our souls.

I want this final chapter to prepare your soul to meet the challenges that await you in your pastoral ministry. When you put down this book and check your e-mail or begin preparing your next sermon, I want it to be well with your soul.

Paul and the Carousel

I think the most effective way I can care for you is to consider with you what happened in Paul's soul as he encountered the challenges of pastoral ministry. Here we will not concentrate on his public ministry, unequalled though that was. We will look here at what took place in the privacy of Paul's heart and at what effect the state of his soul had on his public ministry.

Here is a man whose ministry responsibilities far exceeded our own. He proclaimed the gospel, planted churches, contended for the gospel, and suffered for the gospel. "And, apart from other things, there is the daily pressure on me of my anxiety for all the churches. Who is weak, and I am not weak?" he writes. "Who is made to fall, and I am not indignant?" (2 Cor. 11:28–29)[2]

Paul understood the carousel of ministry responsibility, pressure, and anxiety, no doubt more than any of us. Yet amid his massive responsibilities, look carefully at how he speaks to the Philippian church. The man with the "daily pressure of anxiety for all the churches" writes this:

> I thank my God in all my remembrance of you, always in every prayer of mine for you all making my prayer with joy, because of your partnership in the gospel from the first day until now. And I am sure of this, that he who began a good work in you will bring it to completion at the day of Jesus Christ. It is right for me to feel this way about you all, because I hold you in my heart, for you are all partakers with me of grace, both in my imprisonment and in the defense and confirmation of the gospel. For God is my witness, how I yearn for you all with the affection of Christ Jesus. (Phil. 1:3–8)

In just these few sentences, we see joy-filled gratitude, faith, and affection. And you simply cannot read the rest of the letter without noticing Paul's joy. Philippians is one of Paul's most personal letters, and the dominant emotion of this letter is joy. As R. Kent Hughes has pointed out, the letter as a whole references joy sixteen times, building to a "ringing crescendo" in the command, "Rejoice in the Lord always; again I will say, Rejoice" (4:4).[3] The guy with the most responsibilities is also the happiest guy in the room.

It is all too easy to forget that Paul penned this letter with shackled hands in a Roman prison. Paul was familiar with the carousel. But it wasn't just his ministry responsibilities that set him apart, nor was it simply his suffering and sacrifice for the gospel. What set Paul apart was the *way* he carried all of his pressures and anxieties. He served, he sacrificed, he suffered—and he did it all with joy.

To study this man's life and letters is to encounter this clear characteristic: Paul served the Lord, not just with faithfulness but also with gladness. He was a happy pastor.

Are You a Happy Pastor?

I have no doubt that the overwhelming majority of pastors at Together for the Gospel are serving the Savior and his church faithfully. And for that, each of you has my deepest respect. But I am not certain that the overwhelming majority of pastors are serving the Savior and his church joyfully. I am not sure that all is well with your souls. Faithfulness is both necessary and commendable, but it is not sufficient. If we are to fully please God and accurately represent him, we must also serve our churches joyfully.

So we would be wise to look carefully at Paul's example of joy and to ask ourselves, "Is joy present in my ministry and in my life?"

Please don't misunderstand: I am not speaking of superficial happiness or a cheerful personality. Nor am I denying the reality of sin and suffering, sorrow and tears. But even in times of sorrow and grief, does some degree of joy accompany your sorrow? Even when suffering, Paul described himself as "sorrowful, yet always rejoicing" (2 Cor. 6:10). So do you serve, lead, work, pray, prepare sermons, preach, counsel, and care with a joy obvious to all? Seriously—do you? At the outset of this chapter, let's briefly and humbly evaluate ourselves:

- Would your wife describe you as consistently happy as a pastor, genuinely joyful in the execution of your pastoral responsibilities?
- How would your children describe your demeanor? They are observing you each day; would they say, "My dad is a joyful pastor"?
- What about the pastors or elders serving alongside you? Would they describe you as joyful rather than burdened, moody, often irritable, or easily discouraged?

- What about your assistant, your secretary, or those who serve in administrative roles in the church? What is it like to work with you in a daily routine, outside of public view? Are you consistently joyful, or would they characterize you as busy, hurried, irritated, or demanding?
- Would the members of your congregation say that you are consistently happy, that you are glad to be their pastor?
- What is your church like? Have you built, by your example, a church with a culture of joy? Or perhaps more tangibly, if I were a guest at your church this Sunday, would it be obvious to me that joy characterizes your church?

If you answered all those questions favorably, perhaps you are right—and I hope you are. But you would be wise to confirm your assessment with another, possibly more objective, evaluation. I encourage you to humbly ask your wife, your children, your fellow elders, and your secretary or assistant for their observations. Ask them, "As you watch my life and the way I execute my pastoral responsibilities, am I consistently joyful?"

Most important, what about God? Would he say, "By my grace, because of the gospel, you have served me with gladness"?

From my observation of pastors for more than thirty years, many pastors serve the Lord faithfully but not gladly. Too many faithful pastors appear burdened and discouraged rather than joyful in the execution of their duties. Perhaps you are one of them. You may have been amazed by the preaching and moved by the worship at Together for the Gospel, but in your heart, as you think about your daily life, you are weary, burdened, and perhaps angry. Perhaps you are considering resigning from your church or from the ministry altogether.

If that is you, I want to talk with you. I particularly want to have a word with those who are weary and burdened. And I think one of the most effective ways I can serve you is to draw your attention to the happiest pastor I know of—Paul. The guy with the most responsibilities is also the happiest guy! So the grace of God displayed in the gospel, reflected in Paul's life and ministry, should provide hope for us all, regardless of the state of our soul at present or the challenges that await us on the "carousel of defeat and victory" that is church life.

Paul's Pastoral Ministry

So let's attempt to answer several questions. How did Paul consistently serve the Lord with gladness? What sustained joy in his soul despite hardship, opposition, and responsibility that none of us can relate to? In the shadow of the cross, what can I learn from his example? How can gladness and joy become realities in my life, obvious to my wife, my children, my pastoral team, my secretary, my church members, and even non-Christians?

The answers to these important questions are found in the opening chapter of Philippians. These verses provide us with a window into Paul's soul. As we overhear his divinely inspired words to the Philippian church, we learn how to cultivate and maintain joy amid ministry responsibilities and challenges. This text reveals three characteristics that marked Paul's soul and his pastoral ministry. All three are simple, profound, and easy to assume or neglect. As Paul writes to the Philippians, let's study what happens in his soul. In the process we'll see what will sustain joy in our lives and ministries.

1) Gratitude to God (1:3–5)

In studying Paul's letters, I've become aware of the priority of gratitude in his life and ministry. Apart from our Lord, I don't think there ever was a more grateful man than Paul. His gratitude was sincere, specific, and diverse. In private he gave thanks to God for people and churches, and then he expressed his gratitude in public, written form. The opening verses of this letter are just one example:

"I thank my God in all my remembrance of you, always in every prayer of mine for you all making my prayer with joy, because of your partnership in the gospel from the first day until now" (1:3–5). Paul's expressions of gratefulness to God, and for God's people, are neither subtle nor occasional. They are pronounced and frequent. In fact, it's been written that "Paul mentions the subject of thanksgiving in his letters more often, line for line, than any other Hellenistic author, pagan or Christian."[4]

The expressions of gratitude at the beginning of Philippians are not superficial formalities or mere adherence to ancient etiquette. Nor was Paul's gratitude some unique trait of his pre-conversion personality. His thankfulness was theologically informed. As scholar Peter O'Brien has observed, "Paul's introductory thanksgivings were not meaningless devices. Instead, they were integral parts of their letters, setting the tone and themes of what was to follow."[5] Paul's gratitude, he points out, "is always a response to God's saving activity in creation and redemption."[6]

Scholar David Pao makes similar observations about Paul's writings:

> The grounds [of thanksgiving] are usually acts of God within the lives of the believers and the faithful response of the audience. Thankfulness as a result of the experience of grace by others became a *dominant category*.[7]

Is thankfulness a "dominant category" in our hearts and ministries? If not, it should be.

Paul's habitual gratitude was rooted in theology. It sprang from an awareness of God's grace, of God's activity, and of the gospel's effect and advance. When we discern God's grace in our churches, we too will be grateful to God.

So how grateful are you? What is it like to have a conversation with you? Is it immediately evident that gratefulness is a priority in your pastoral ministry? Have you created in your church a culture of gratitude that is plain to anyone who visits? If not, perhaps you don't share Paul's conviction about the importance of gratitude.

If gratitude does not characterize you, I encourage you to study this topic in Paul's life and to discover its life-altering relevance for your soul and your ministry. You will experience God's transforming grace for the sake of your family, for your church, and ultimately for the advance of the gospel of Jesus Christ. And you will avoid becoming vulnerable to the subtle, serious, and predictable sin of complaining.

I want to prepare you for this temptation, because pastoral ministry provides countless daily opportunities to complain, and from my experience, many of us do not realize the seriousness of this sin. I know I was unaware.

MY NOT-SO-INSIGNIFICANT SIN

A number of years ago, my friend David Powlison taught the Dynamics of Biblical Change course to Covenant Life Church, where I was pastoring. In his opening session, David suggested that we choose just one area of our lives to address during the course, so we would not be overwhelmed by the day-long deluge of information that was to follow. As an example, David volunteered the topic of complaining and began to illustrate it from his life. Rather than thinking creatively, I adopted his topic. Throughout the seminar and in the weeks and months that followed, I focused on the area of complaining and began to seek biblical change. Little did I know what was providentially underway in my life.

What David Powlison inadvertently set in motion for me was a two-year study of the topic of complaining in Scripture and in my life. I gave more careful attention to familiar passages such as Numbers 11 and 1 Corinthians 10 and supplemented this study with the works of Puritans such as Jeremiah Burroughs and Thomas Watson.[8]

As I studied the sin of complaining, I soon realized it was as subtle as it was pervasive. It colored not only my speech but my behavior as well. And I discovered something even more serious: my complaints weren't innocent statements of how I felt about my circumstances, uttered in complete privacy, with no consequences. When I complained, I had an audience. I was complaining against some*one*: God himself.

The unexpected discovery that impressed upon me the serious-ness of my sin was this: complaining reveals the pride in my heart. God is not indifferent to my complaints, for when I complain, I am wise in my own eyes. I am arrogantly challenging God's wisdom. As Thomas Watson puts it, "Murmuring . . . is a rising up against God."[9] Why is this? "For thou settest thyself above God . . . as if thou wert wiser than he."[10] And if you aren't feeling this yet, I dare you to read these words from John Calvin without experiencing some degree of conviction:

> Why is it that men fret so when God sends them things entirely contrary to their desires except that they do not acknowledge that God does everything by reason and that He has just cause? . . .
>
> As soon as God does not send what we have desired, we dis-pute against Him, we bring suit, not that we appear to do this, but our manner shows that this is nevertheless our intent. . . . But from what spirit is this pronounced? From a poisoned heart; as if we said, "The thing should have been otherwise, *I see no reason for this*." Meanwhile God will be condemned among us. This is how men exasperate themselves. And in this what do they do? It is as if they accused God of being a tyrant or a hairbrain who asked only to put everything in confusion. Such horrible blasphemy blows out of the mouths of men.[11]

I vividly remember the first time I read those words, and they have been guarding my soul ever since.

How often during the day I am tempted to complain about hardships, whether trivial or severe. Each time, the pride in my heart says, "I see no reason for this." When I complain, I am calling into question the sovereignty, wisdom, and goodness of God. Trouble? Sorrow? Inconvenience? *I see no reason for this.* "Such horrible blasphemy blows out of the mouths of men." It was blowing out of my mouth daily.

So how do you respond to tests of adversity, perplexing circumstances, criticism, or suffering? As you put this book down and receive a discouraging phone call, or the next time you are criticized after preaching a sermon, what will happen in your soul? The occasions for complaining are endless, and each time you will be tempted to say, "I see no reason for this." When we respond to difficulty in this way, we are in our arrogance, presuming to be wiser than God.

CULTIVATING GRATITUDE

One primary way to weaken the sin of complaining is to cultivate gratitude for the many evidences of God's grace in your church. Paul could be grateful for the Philippian church because he perceived God's activity among them. The church, while impressive, was in need of adjustment. Pride and selfish ambition were threatening to undermine its unity. Two church members were in conflict with each other. Yet Paul was more aware of God's grace than of their deficiencies.

He begins this letter by reviewing God's work for, within, and through this church. He gives thanks for all of them, praying for them with joy "because of your partnership in the gospel from the first day until now," which it appears he vividly remembered (vv. 4–5). In these opening verses, as we overhear how Paul prayed for this church, the sound is one of joyful gratitude to God for his grace at work in them.

If we were to listen in on your prayers, what would we hear? Would it be the sound of specific, sincere, joyful thanksgiving to God for your church? You will find a direct correlation: where you lack joy, complaining has replaced gratitude. When you are discouraged, you are more aware of your church's deficiencies than of evidences of God's grace. If that is you, gospel-informed gratitude will alter your soul and change your pastoral ministry dramatically.

A grateful heart will affect your preaching. It's easy to discern the difference between a grateful pastor and a self-righteous or irritated pastor in his tone and demeanor.

A grateful heart will affect your counseling. If, before you begin counseling, you remind yourself of God's grace in that person's life, you will be freshly grateful for him. As you counsel, your gratefulness will be obvious, and you will transfer the hope of the gospel to him in that conversation.

A grateful heart will affect your relationship with the leaders in your church. You will view them as brothers and friends and co-laborers, gifts from God, not as professional colleagues or a means of sanctification.

A grateful heart will affect your wife, protecting her from bitterness, offense, and discouragement. A grateful heart will affect how your children view your church. What do your children hear from you about the church? Do they hear criticism and complaining, or thankfulness? When they hear you celebrate God's grace in your church rather than complain, they will be protected from bitterness or offense.

A grateful heart, as you model and teach it, will affect your church. Every Sunday, God's grace is evident throughout your church in countless ways because of the gospel of Jesus Christ. Teach your church to see and celebrate these evidences of grace and to glorify God for them. Model and teach this, and you will create and cultivate a culture of gratitude.

Gratitude was, as Pao writes, a "dominant category" for Paul. Resolve, by God's grace, to make gratitude a dominant category in your life, and you will be a joyful pastor—and most importantly, you will please and glorify God.

2) Faith toward God (1:6)

What other explanations do we find for Paul's gladness despite ministry challenges and hardships? How could he write to the Philippians, "I thank my God in all my remembrance of you, always in every prayer of mine for you all making my prayer with joy" (1:3–4)? The second explanation for Paul's pronounced joy, the reason he could serve the Lord with both faithfulness and gladness, was faith. *"And I am sure of this,"* he writes, "that he who began a good work in you will bring it to completion at the day of Jesus Christ" (1:6).

Trust in God, in his promises and purpose, informed Paul's service. He was confident that God would fulfill his purpose for this church through the gospel of Jesus Christ. His confidence in the Philippians' future was rooted in their past—in the One who had begun this good work. He knew that this church had begun with the effectual call of God, through the proclamation of the gospel. Paul was sure of this: what God begins, he sustains and completes.

This is impressive confidence from a guy chained to the wall of a Roman prison. Sometimes, even sitting in the comfort of an elders' meeting, I am *not* sure. How can we share this confidence? Our confidence for those entrusted to our care should be no different from Paul's. If the members of your church are regenerated—if they have turned from their sin and trusted in the Savior as a substitutionary sacrifice for their sin—they are no different from the Philippians. So you can and should share Paul's certainty about God's work in their hearts and lives. This faith toward God for your church will change your perspective of your church and your ministry. It will even change the way you speak to your church.

Paul's confidence for the church was rooted in theology, not in a naturally optimistic outlook. And the same theological information—leading to the same confidence—is available to you.

WANT OF FAITH

If you, pastor, aren't confident in God for those entrusted to your care, I encourage you to set aside a season of time for a fresh study of the nature of faith and its importance as you cultivate joy in your pastoral ministry. Let me recommend that you allow the nineteenth-century pastor Charles Bridges (1794–1869) to assist you in this study. His book *The Christian Ministry* is outstanding—it has been the second-most influential book in my pastoral ministry[12]—and especially one short chapter titled "Want of Faith," which you must not only read, but memorize. In this chapter Bridges writes:

> All our failures may be ultimately traced to a defect of faith. . . . The life of faith, therefore, is the life of the Minister's work and the spring of his success. . . .
>
> The main difficulty, therefore, is not in our work, but in ourselves; in the conflict with our own unbelief. . . . Difficulties heaped upon difficulties can never rise to the level of the promise of God. . . .
>
> It is faith that enlivens our work with perpetual cheerfulness. It commits every part of it to God, in the hope, that even mistakes shall be overruled for his glory; and thus relieves us from an oppressive anxiety, often attendant upon a deep sense of our responsibility. The shortest way to peace will be found in casting ourselves upon God for daily pardon of deficiencies and supplies of grace, without looking too eagerly for present fruit. Hence our course of effort is unvarying, but more tranquil. . . . Unbelief looks at the difficulty. Faith regards the promise. Unbelief therefore makes our work a service of bondage. Faith realizes it as a "labour of love." Unbelief drags on in sullen despondency. Faith makes the patience, with which it is content to wait for success, "the patience of hope" [1 Thess. 1:3 KJV]. As every difficulty . . . is the fruit of unbelief; so will they all ultimately be overcome by the perseverance of faith.[13]

The primary difficulty is not in our work; it is within us. "All our failures," Bridges says, "may be ultimately traced to a defect of faith." Surely not *all* of them? Yes: every one.

Rare is the day that this passage doesn't have some influence on my soul. Since reading this, I have sought to make the life of faith the life of my work, and I have grown to understand that my daily difficulty is never the work. It is my unbelief. I have learned that when I lack joy and ministry is, or appears, difficult, my soul is giving way to unbelief. As Bridges says, "It is faith that enlivens our work with perpetual cheerfulness."

So is your pastoral ministry marked by perpetual cheerfulness? If not, Bridges has a simple but profound diagnosis: what you need is *faith*. In fact, you cannot please God, or by implication pastor effectively, without faith toward God. There are no substitutes for faith. Without it, Hebrews 11:6 tells us, it is not merely difficult to please God; it is *impossible*.

NO BETTER GOSPEL

Where is your confidence when you stand behind the sacred desk to preach? Is it in the One who began a good work and will sustain and complete it, using the preaching of his Word as a means to do this? Are you trusting in your eloquence, relevance, awareness of culture, or humor? Or is your confidence in the power of God to transform lives through the proclamation of the gospel?

While at Together for the Gospel, listening to world-class teachers, observing their exceptional gifts, and feeling the effect of their preaching, it's easy to think, "I can't do that." Let me confirm your discernment: you can't. Neither can I. Only a few can preach like they do. But if that discourages you, your confidence is misplaced. If your confidence is in your gifting, your education, your preparation, your eloquence, or your wit, then it is not in the One who began this good work. Our confidence must be in the gospel we proclaim.

Spurgeon captured this in a characteristically witty statement to his Pastors College students: "Your ministry is poor enough. Everybody knows that, and you ought to know it most of all."[14]

You have got to love hearing that from your mentor in ministry. "Your ministry is pathetic, and everybody knows it. You ought to know it most of all."

But he went on to remind his students that their preaching was effective only because God keeps his promise. "So shall my word be that goes out from my mouth; it shall not return to me empty, but it shall accomplish that which I purpose, and shall succeed in the thing for which I sent it" (Isa. 55:11). You can step into your pulpit this Sunday with confidence in God and in his promise for your church.

On another occasion Spurgeon said, "Whitefield and Wesley might preach the gospel better than I do, but they could not preach a better gospel."[15] I would paraphrase Spurgeon like this: Mark Dever, Ligon Duncan, Al Mohler, Thabiti Anyabwile, John MacArthur, John Piper, R. C. Sproul—they all preach the gospel better than I can. But the good news for me, and for all of us, is this: they cannot preach a better gospel.

This should bring joy to all average pastors. As you approach your pulpit this Sunday, go in the confidence that God will continue the good work he has begun in your church through the proclamation of the gospel. And let this faith enliven your work with perpetual cheerfulness.

3) Affection for Others (1:7–8)

As we overhear Paul's words to the Philippian church, there is one more explanation for the consistent joy in his soul. How could he pray, preach, write, and serve and do all this with gladness? How did he avoid discouragement as he faced the challenges of pastoral ministry?

The third source of Paul's joy is found in a verse that is easy to overlook. This statement is stunning: "God is my witness, how I *yearn* for you all *with the affection of Christ Jesus*" (1:8). Paul cared for this church with the very affection of Christ himself. This kind of love permeates Paul's ministry and letters. This was not because Paul was naturally a relational guy, a "people person." It was not a personality issue. We find the explanation for his affection in verse 7: "For you are all partakers with me of grace." Paul's affection for the Philippians had a theological basis. It was rooted not in personality but in the gospel. Each church Paul planted and served was the object of his affection, because each was the object of Christ Jesus' affection.

Paul's statement is both a challenge to us and a source of hope. By the grace of God, we actually can care for those in our churches with the affection the Savior has for them. The gospel, understood and applied, creates affection for those whom the Savior bought with his own blood.

So how do you feel about those you serve? Could you say that you feel this affection for them—for *all* of them? Or do you view your role as merely preaching to them? Are you irritated with certain members of your church, or perhaps indifferent to large segments of its population? Is your church more aware of your correction or your affection? If, when you consider your church, you do not find affection in your heart for them, do not rest until you find out why. Cultivating love for God's people must be a priority for pastors. Members of our churches must encounter the affection of Christ through our conversations, prayer, encouragement, counseling, and preaching.

When I don't feel this love for somebody, it's usually because I have lost sight of Christ's love for him. I find that a simple practice renews my affection: I contemplate Christ's death on the cross for him. I follow the wise counsel of Charles Spurgeon and "dwell where the cries of Calvary can be heard."[16] The Savior loved this person enough to bear the wrath of God on his behalf. As I consider the amazing affection of Christ for him, affection is reignited in my soul.

At some point each of us will grow tired of caring for our

churches. If you are weary, I commend to you an extended season of surveying the wondrous cross, contemplating the Savior's love for your church. Only by the contemplation of Calvary can your affection be refreshed and sustained. As you consider Christ's death for those in your church, by the grace of God, your heart will be filled with love for them—not superficial feelings or an expression of your personality, but the very affection of Jesus Christ. If Paul were here, I think he would say to us, "Pay careful attention to yourselves and to all the flock, in which the Holy Spirit has made you overseers, *to care for the church of God, which he obtained with his own blood*" (Acts 20:28). There is an inseparable relationship between your affection for the church and your contemplation of Calvary.

When you stand at your pulpit this Sunday looking out over your church, say to yourself, "I address those whom he obtained through his own blood. These are those for whom the Savior died. Our Lord cried out, 'My God, my God, why have you forsaken me?' for those I am about to address" (Matt. 27:46). Never attempt to care for your church apart from an awareness that Christ died for them.

And as this love grows in your soul, seize every occasion to express it to them! Cultivate affection for your church as you pray and prepare your sermons. Express it as you greet the people in your church on a Sunday morning. Never correct your church or an individual member of it if your heart lacks affection for them.

As you gaze upon the wondrous cross, as you consider the affection of Christ for the people you serve, your affections will be transformed. Your church will become to you, as Spurgeon once described it, "the dearest place on earth."

Conclusion

The Together for the Gospel conference (and by extension, the essays in this book) was intended to refresh and equip us for our primary work: serving local churches. We are called to stay on the carousel where our challenge is maintaining joy over the long haul. But we can be certain that what sustained Paul will sustain us. Like Paul, we have every reason to be grateful to God. We have every reason to trust God, every reason to love those for whom the Savior died.

What a privilege it is to be a pastor. We have every reason to be joyful pastors.

NOTES

Introduction

1. C. H. Spurgeon, *Autobiography* (London: Passmore and Alabaster, 1898), 2:86.

2. Martin Luther, *On the Bondage of the Will*, trans. Philip S. Watson, in *Luther and Erasmus: Free Will and Salvation*, ed. E. Gordon Rupp and Philip S. Watson (Philadelphia: Westminster Press, 1969), 105–6.

Chapter 1: Sound Doctrine

1. Eerdmans is producing a new edition with an introduction by Carl Trueman, who is professor of historical theology and church history at Westminster Theological Seminary in Philadelphia.

2. Valerie Cohen, "The Dangers of Theology: Jews Focus More on Deed than Creed," *Clarion Ledger*, April 12, 2008.

3. Ibid.

4. Ibid.

5. Ibid.

6. Mark Dever, *Nine Marks of a Healthy Church*, rev. and exp. ed. (Wheaton, IL: Crossway, 2000), 57.

7. Eugene D. Genovese, *The Southern Tradition: The Achievement and Limitations of an American Conservatism* (Cambridge, MA: Harvard University Press, 1994).

8. Scot McKnight, "Five Streams of the Emerging Church," *Christianity Today*, February 2007, in Collin Hansen, *Young, Restless, Reformed: A Journalist's Journey with the New Calvinists* (Wheaton, IL: Crossway, 2008), 151.

9. Unless otherwise indicated, Scripture references in this chapter are from the ESV.

10. Carl Trueman, "Bring Me My Broadsword," *The Monthly Record* 12 (October 2008): 12.

11. Bruce K. Waltke, *An Old Testament Theology: An Exegetical, Canonical, and Thematic Approach* (Grand Rapids: Zondervan, 2007), 31.

12. Ibid., 64.

13. Donald Macleod, *The Humiliated and Exalted Lord: Studies in Philippians 2 and Christology* (Greenville, SC: Reformed Academic Press, 1994), 4.

14. Introduction to Martin Luther, *The Bondage of the Will*, trans. J. I. Packer and O. R. Johnston (Grand Rapids: Revell, 1957), 44.

15. Norval Geldenhuys, *Commentary on the Gospel of Luke* (Grand Rapids: Eerdmans, 1954), 634.

16. Wayne Grudem, *Systematic Theology: An Introduction to Biblical Doctrine* (Grand Rapids: Zondervan, 1994), 23.

17. I am indebted to Donald Macleod for his wonderful article "The Doctrine of God and Pastoral Care," in *Engaging the Doctrine of God: Contemporary Protestant Perspectives*, ed. Bruce McCormack (Grand Rapids: Baker Academic, 2008), 245–60.

Chapter 2: Bearing the Image

1. Unless otherwise indicated, Scripture references in this chapter are from the ESV.

2. For an excellent review of the history of race theory, science, and the Bible, see Collin Kidd, *The Forging of Races: Race and Scripture in the Protestant Atlantic World, 1600–2000* (Cambridge, UK: Cambridge University Press, 2006).

3. Ibid. For other recent studies that abandon race as a viable biological category, see D. G. Blackburn, "Why Race Is Not a Biological Concept," in *Race and Racism in Theory and Practice*, ed. B. Lang (Lanham, MD: Rowman and Littlefield, 2000), 11–12; A. F. Corcos, *The Myth of Human Races* (East Lansing, MI: Michigan State University Press, 1997).

4. See, e.g., L. Long and R. A. Kittles, "Human Genetic Variation and the Nonexistence of Human Races," *Human Biology* 75, no. 4 (2003): 449–71; A. Smedley and B. D. Smedley, "Race as Biology Is Fiction, Racism as a Social Problem Is Real: Anthropological and Historical Perspectives on the Social Construction of Race," *American Psychologist* 60, no. 1 (January 2005): 16–26.

5. I realize that some people may use the term *race* in the way I am using *ethnicity*, a fluid social construct that is not determined by biology. If in that sense a person uses *race* as a synonym for *ethnicity*, then I would have little disagreement with the use of *race*. However, that use of *race* would be incon-

sistent with the historical and contemporary use of the term where, at least in part, essential biological distinctiveness is thought to determine a person's racial grouping.

6. Kidd, *The Forging of Races*, 21.

7. Sinclair Ferguson, *In Christ Alone: Living the Gospel-centered Life* (Lake Mary, FL: Reformation Trust, 2007), 157.

Chapter 3: The Sinner Neither Willing nor Able

1. Unless otherwise indicated, Scripture references in this chapter are from the NASB.

Chapter 4: Improving the Gospel

1. Unless otherwise indicated, Scripture references in this chapter are from the NIV.

2. Al Hsu, "A Multifaceted Gospel," *Christianity Today*, April 2008, 66.

3. Tom Wright, *Surprised by Hope* (London: SPCK, 2007), 266, cited in *Christianity Today*, April 2008.

4. See Tom Wright, *Paul for Everyone: 1 Corinthians* (Louisville, KY: Westminster John Knox, 2004), 28.

5. For more on this, see Greg Gilbert's addendum immediately following this chapter.

6. Charles Colson, in *UnChristian: What a New Generation Really Thinks about Christianity . . . and Why It Matters*, ed. David Kinnaman and Gabe Lyons (Grand Rapids: Baker, 2007), 87.

7. Rick Warren, *The Purpose-Driven Church: Growth without Compromising Your Message and Mission* (Grand Rapids: Zondervan, 1995), 142, 256–57.

8. Ibid., 280.

9. Jonathan Edwards, "The Church's Marriage to Her Sons, and to Her God," *Works*, 25.187.

Addendum: What Is the Gospel?

1. Unless otherwise indicated, Scripture references in this chapter are from the ESV.

Chapter 5: The Curse Motif of the Atonement

1. Unless otherwise indicated, Scripture references in this chapter are from the ESV.

Chapter 6: Why They Hate It So

1. Harry Fosdick, "Shall the Fundamentalists Win?" http://historymatters. gmu.edu/d/5070/ (accessed January 16, 2009).

2. J. I. Packer, "What Did the Cross Achieve? The Logic of Penal Substitution," in *In My Place Condemned He Stood: Celebrating the Glory of the Atonement*, ed. J. I. Packer and Mark Dever (Wheaton, IL: Crossway, 2007), 53.

3. J. I. Packer, "Penal Substitution Revisited," in *In My Place Condemned He Stood*, ed. Packer and Dever, 21.

4. Peter Steinfels, "Cries of Heresy after Feminists Meet," *New York Times*, May 14, 1994.

5. Abby Noll, "Herstory and Heresy: A Womanist/Feminist Perspective on Jesus," Voices of Orthodox Women, http://www.vow.org/feminism/ contemporary.issues/xxxxxxx-noll-herstory_and_heresy.html (accessed January 16, 2009).

6. Ibid.

7. Unless otherwise indicated, Scripture references in this chapter are from the ESV.

8. J. I. Packer, "What Did the Cross Achieve?" in *In My Place Condemned He Stood*, ed. Packer and Dever, 71–73.

9. Mark Dever, "Nothing but the Blood," *Christianity Today*, May 2006.

10. Mark Dever, "Nothing but the Blood," in *In My Place Condemned He Stood*, ed. Packer and Dever, 102–3.

11. I. Howard Marshall, "Some Thoughts on Penal Substitution," *Irish Biblical Studies* 26, no. 3 (2005): 122–23.

12. C. H. Dodd, *The Apostolic Preaching and Its Developments* (London: Hodder and Stoughton, 1964).

13. Leon Morris, *The Apostolic Preaching of the Cross* (London: Tyndale Press, 1955).

14. Clark H. Pinnock and Robert C. Brow, *Unbounded Love: A Good News Theology for the 21st Century* (Downers Grove, IL: InterVarsity, 1994), 102.

15. Ibid., 103.

16. John Stott, *The Cross of Christ* (Downers Grove, IL: InterVarsity, 1986), 159.

17. Joel Green and Mark Baker, *Recovering the Scandal of the Cross: Atonement in New Testament and Contemporary Contexts* (Downers Grove, IL: InterVarsity, 2000).

18. Steve Chalke and Alan Mann, *The Lost Message of Jesus* (Grand Rapids: Zondervan, 2004), 182.

19. http://www.eauk.org/about/basis-of-faith.cfm.

20. Ibid.

21. Steve Jeffery, Michael Ovey, and Andrew Sach, *Pierced for Our Transgressions: Rediscovering the Glory of Penal Substitution* (Wheaton, IL: Crossway, 2007), 22.

22. For more on this subject, see D. A. Carson, *Becoming Conversant with the Emergent Church: Understanding a Movement and Its Implications* (Grand Rapids: Zondervan, 2005); Kevin DeYoung and Ted Kluck, *Why We're Not Emergent (By Two Guys Who Should Be)* (Chicago: Moody, 2008).

23. Chalke and Mann, *The Lost Message of Jesus*, 122–37.

24. Walter Wink, *Engaging the Powers: Discernment and Resistance in a World of Domination* (Minneapolis: Fortress Press, 1992), 13–31.

25. Pinnock and Brow, *Unbounded Love*, 102.

26. Ibid., 102–3.

27. Ibid., 103.

28. Ibid.

29. Green and Baker, *Recovering the Scandal of the Cross*, 202.

30. Ibid., 203.

31. Donald Capps, *The Child's Song: The Religious Abuse of Children* (Louisville, KY: Westminster John Knox, 1995).

32. René Girard, *The Scapegoat*, trans. Yvonne Freccero (Baltimore: Johns Hopkins University Press, 1986); *Things Hidden Since the Foundation of the World*, trans. Stephen Bann and Michael Metteer (repr., Palo Alto: Stanford University Press, 1987); *Violence and the Sacred* (New York: Continuum, 2005).

33. David Van Biema, "Why Did Jesus Die?" *Time*, April 12, 2004, 60.

34. Sally Brown, *Cross Talk* (Louisville, KY: Westminster John Knox, 2008).

Chapter 7: The Supremacy of Christ and Radical Christian Sacrifice

1. Unless otherwise indicated, Scripture references in this chapter are from the ESV.

2. Howard Guinness, *Sacrifice* (1936), in Lindsay Brown, *Shining Like Stars: The Power of the Gospel in the World's Universities* (Nottingham, UK: Inter-Varsity, 2006), 151.

3. Ibid., 160–61.

4. Compare the uses of the phrase "word of exhortation" in Hebrews 13:22 and in Acts 13:15. Dennis Johnson, *Him We Proclaim: Preaching Christ from All the Scriptures* (Phillipsburg, NJ: P&R, 2007), 172.

5. Observe in Hebrews 10:34 that the word translated "property" (*huparchonton*) has the same Greek root (in the plural) as the word translated "possession" (*huparxin*). A more literal rendering would read: "You received with joy the plunder of your *possessions* (plural), knowing yourselves to have a better and lasting *possession* (singular)." They joyfully accepted the loss of their earthly, plural possessions because they knew that they had a superior singular possession, namely, Jesus.

Chapter 8: Sustaining the Pastor's Soul

1. Pete Alwinson, "Already, but Not Yet," *Tabletalk* 19, no. 1 (January 1995), 54. Scripture quotations are from the NKJV.

2. Unless otherwise indicated, Scripture references in this chapter are from the ESV.

3. R. Kent Hughes, *Philippians: The Fellowship of the Gospel* (Wheaton, IL: Crossway, 2007), 25.

4. Gerald F. Hawthorne, Ralph P. Martin, and Daniel G. Reid, eds., *Dictionary of Paul and His Letters* (Downers Grove, IL: InterVarsity, 1993), 69.

5. Peter O'Brien, *Introductory Thanksgivings in the Letters of Paul* (Leiden: E. J. Brill, 1977), 263.

6. Peter O'Brien, "Thanksgiving within the Structure of Pauline Theology," in *Pauline Studies: Essays Presented to Professor F. F. Bruce on His 70th Birthday*, ed. D. A. Hagner and M. J. Harris (Grand Rapids: Eerdmans, 1980), 62.

7. David W. Pao, *Thanksgiving: An Investigation of a Pauline Theme* (Downers Grove, IL: InterVarsity, 2002), 20; emphasis added.

8. I highly recommend *The Rare Jewel of Christian Contentment* by Jeremiah Burroughs (Carlisle, PA: Banner of Truth, 1964) and *The Art of Divine Contentment* by Thomas Watson (London: Religious Tract Society, 1835; repr. Morgan, PA: Soli Deo Gloria, 2001).

9. Watson, *The Art of Divine Contentment*, 30.

10. Ibid., *iv*.

11. John Calvin, *Sermons from Job*, trans. Leroy Nixon (Grand Rapids: Eerdmans, 1952), 29–30, quoted in Robert D. Jones, "Anger against God," *Journal of Biblical Counseling* 14, no. 3 (Spring 1996): 17; emphasis added.

12. The most influential has been *The Cross and Christian Ministry: Leadership Lessons from 1 Corinthians* by D. A. Carson (Grand Rapids: Baker, 2004).

13. Charles Bridges, *The Christian Ministry: With an Inquiry into the Causes of Its Inefficiency* (Edinburgh: Banner of Truth, 1830; 1991), 173–75, 178–79.

14. Spurgeon, "The Holy Spirit in Connection with Our Ministry," in *Lectures to My Students* (London: Marshall, Morgan and Scott, 1954), 194.

15. Charles Spurgeon, *The Metropolitan Pulpit: 1882*, vol. 28 (Pasadena, TX: Pilgrim, 1973), 339.

16. Charles Spurgeon, "To Lovers of Jesus" (sermon, Metropolitan Tabernacle, London, August 8, 1886).

NAME INDEX

SCRIPTURE INDEX